A Pinch of This, A Dash of That

Gooseberry Patch

**An imprint of
The Globe Pequot Publishing Group, Inc.
64 South Main Street
Essex, CT 06426**

www.gooseberrypatch.com

1•800•854•6673

Copyright 2024, Gooseberry Patch 978-1-62093-585-9

Photo Edition is a major revision of **A Pinch of This, A Dash of That**.

Do you have a tried & true recipe...

tip, craft or memory that you'd like to see featured in a **Gooseberry Patch** cookbook? Visit our website at **www.gooseberrypatch.com** and follow the easy steps to submit your favorite family recipe.

Or send them to us at:

Gooseberry Patch
PO Box 812
Columbus, OH 43216-0812

Don't forget to include the number of servings your recipe makes, plus your name, address, phone number and email address. If we select your recipe, your name will appear right along with it...and you'll receive a **FREE** copy of the book!

Contents

Farmhouse Breakfasts 5

Old-Fashioned Breads 27

Simmering Soups 51

Patchwork Salads 77

Family-style Casseroles . . . 101

Hometown Main Dishes 125

Country Sides 153

Grandma's Baked Goods . . . 185

DEDICATION

For everyone who celebrates the sweet memories of Grandma's cooking.

APPRECIATION

Thanks to our wonderful friends, for sharing your heart-felt memories and favorite recipes!

Farmhouse Breakfasts

Growing up, my sister and I spent many weekends at our grandparents' farm...wintry Saturday mornings were always our favorite! While we were still warmly tucked under several quilts, Grandpa was up early on those frosty mornings feeding animals and milking cows. Up just as early, Grandma could be found puttering in the kitchen, and before long we would wake up to the smell of sizzling sausage and fresh coffee.

We'd quickly dress and run downstairs to be greeted by a table set with biscuits, sausage gravy, home fries, eggs and homemade bread with fresh butter! We always ate a hearty breakfast; Grandpa said we needed it to give us energy for the day's chores.

Now, many years later, my family enjoys the same hearty breakfast on chilly Saturday mornings. As I listen to the gusty wind whistling through the pines, I realize we never outgrow our need for simplicity and family traditions.

Buttermilk-Chocolate Muffins

Marion Herman
Topeka, KS

Stir in some chocolate or peanut butter chips for variety.

1-3/4 c. all-purpose flour
3 T. baking cocoa
3 T. brown sugar, packed
3 T. sugar
2-1/2 t. baking powder

1/2 t. baking soda
1/2 t. salt
1 c. buttermilk
2 eggs, beaten

Mix all dry ingredients together. In a separate bowl, combine buttermilk and eggs. Make a well in the center of dry ingredients and pour in buttermilk mixture. Mix until just moistened. Spoon into a greased muffin pan and bake at 400 degrees for 15 minutes. Makes about one dozen.

A collection of old buttons or spools will look great in one of Grandma's glass canning jars. Try to find jars with tin or zinc lids for a real old-fashioned feel.

Grammy Irene's Sticky Buns

Cindy Johnston-Bumar
Loyalhanna, PA

*I remember my sister and I standing with our mouths watering when
Mom would make these. Eat them warm from the oven;
there's nothing better!*

1/3 c. milk	1/4 c. very warm water,
1/4 c. sugar	110 to 115 degrees
1/2 t. salt	1 egg, beaten
1/4 c. butter	2-1/2 c. all-purpose flour,
1 pkg. active dry yeast	divided

In a small saucepan, heat milk until bubbles form around edge of pan.
Remove from heat. Add sugar, salt and butter. Stir to melt; cool to
lukewarm. Sprinkle yeast over water in a large bowl. Stir to dissolve.
Stir in lukewarm milk mixture. Add egg and 2 cups flour. Beat with an
electric mixer until smooth. Add remaining flour and mix by hand until
dough is smooth and leaves the sides of the bowl. Turn dough onto
lightly floured pastry cloth. Knead until dough is smooth and blisters
appear. Place in a lightly greased large bowl, turning to bring greased
side up. Cover with towel. Let rise in a warm place, free from drafts
until double in size, about one to 1-1/2 hours.

Filling:

1/2 c. butter, softened and	1/2 c. chopped pecans or
divided	walnut halves
1 c. brown sugar, packed	1/2 c. raisins
and divided	1/2 t. cinnamon

Blend 1/4 cup butter and 1/2 cup brown sugar. Spread on bottom and
sides of 9"x9" baking pan. Sprinkle butter mixture with nuts. Roll
dough on lightly floured surface into a 16"x12" rectangle. Spread with
remaining butter and brown sugar. Sprinkle with raisins and
cinnamon. Roll up long side, pinching edges to seal. Cut crosswise into
12 slices and place cut-side down in pan. Let rise, covered, in a warm
place until doubled. Bake at 375 degrees for 30 minutes or until
golden. Invert on board; let stand for one minute, then remove from
pan. Makes one dozen.

Popover Pancake

Karen Pilcher
Burleson, TX

Enjoy this extra large puffy pancake with a hot mug of tea.

1/2 c. all-purpose flour	1/4 c. butter
1/2 c. milk	2 t. powdered sugar
2 eggs, beaten	juice of 1/2 lemon

In a mixing bowl, beat together flour, milk and eggs until slightly lumpy. Melt butter in a 9"x9" baking pan and then pour in the batter. Bake at 350 degrees for 20 minutes, until puffy. Sprinkle powdered sugar and lemon juice over pancake, and return to oven for 2 to 3 minutes. Cut into squares. Serves 4.

Old berry pails are beautiful filled to the brim with rosehips; you can even tuck a votive inside!

Apple Fritters

Joanne West
Beavercreek, OH

An Ohio favorite!

1 c. all-purpose flour
1-1/2 t. baking powder
2 T. sugar
1/2 t. salt
1 egg, beaten

1/2 c. plus 1 T. milk
1-1/2 c. apples, peeled, cored
   and diced
oil for frying

Sift dry ingredients together. Whisk together egg and milk; pour into dry ingredients and stir until batter is smooth. Add apples to batter and blend well. Add enough oil to equal one inch deep in a heavy skillet. Drop batter by spoonfuls in hot oil and fry until golden on both sides. For a quicker version, core and slice the apples in rings, dip in batter and fry until golden. Serves 4 to 6.

Enjoy the little things, for one day
you may look back and realize
they were the big things.

–Robert Brault

Orange Breakfast Crescents

Teresa Sullivan
Westerville, OH

Enjoy these warm while the icing is still melting!

3-oz. pkg. cream cheese
3 T. sugar
1/4 t. almond extract

1 t. orange zest, grated
1 pkg. 8-count refrigerated
   crescent rolls

Blend first 4 ingredients. Separate rolls into triangles. Divide cheese mixture among dough triangles, spread, leaving a 1/4-inch border. Roll each, starting at the long edge. Place on lightly greased baking sheet, shaping into crescents. Bake at 350 degrees for 15 minutes or until lightly browned.

Topping:

1/2 c. powdered sugar
1 T. orange juice
1 t. orange zest

1 t. margarine, melted
1/8 t. almond extract

Combine all ingredients while rolls are baking. Spread over hot crescent rolls and serve immediately. Makes 8 crescents.

Antique quilts that are torn, can still be used!
They make wonderful table runners, doll quilts
or Christmas tree skirts.

Sweetheart Muffins

Kimberly McDole
Sparta, NJ

*Make someone you love feel special...serve these muffins in
a basket lined with an embroidered handkerchief.*

6 T. butter
3/4 c. sugar
2 eggs, beaten
1/2 c. milk
2 c. strawberries, rinsed and
   stems removed

2 c. all-purpose flour
1/4 t. salt
1 T. baking powder
milk chocolate drops or your
   favorite flavor of jam

In a large bowl, blend together butter and sugar. Mix in the eggs,
one at a time; add the milk. Mash the berries or purée in blender. Stir
the berries into butter mixture. In a separate bowl, sift flour, salt and
baking powder. Stir well. Add the flour mixture to the berry mixture.
Use a wooden spoon to stir. Line a muffin tin with paper liners. Drop
the batter from a tablespoon to fill the cups halfway. Add a sweet
surprise: a milk chocolate drop, or 1/2 teaspoon of jam. Then spoon
more batter and fill almost to the top. Bake at 350 degrees until the
muffins begin to brown and a toothpick inserted near the center
comes out clean, about 20 to 25 minutes. Remove muffins
from tin and cool. Makes one dozen muffins.

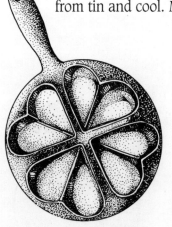

All happiness depends on
a leisurely breakfast.

– John Gunther

Amish Sweet Rolls

Jo Ann
Gooseberry Patch

Frost these rolls with your favorite powdered sugar icing, if desired. Best with an icy cold glass of milk!

1 pkg. active dry yeast	1 c. milk, scalded, or
1/4 c. very warm water,	1 c. hot water
110 to 115 degrees	1 t. salt
1/4 c. plus 1 T. shortening,	3-1/4 to 4 c. all-purpose flour
divided	1 egg, beaten
1/4 c. sugar	

Dissolve yeast in warm water. In a large bowl, combine 1/4 cup shortening and sugar. Pour hot milk or water over mixture. Cool to lukewarm. Blend salt into flour. Add one cup of flour to sugar mixture and beat well. Beat in yeast mixture and egg. Gradually add remaining flour to form soft dough, beating well. Brush top of dough with remaining shortening. Cover and let rise in warm place until doubled, about one to 2 hours. Punch down and knead. Divide dough in half. Roll each half into a rectangle approximately 12 inches by 8 inches.

Filling:

1/4 c. butter	1 t. cinnamon
1/2 c. brown sugar, packed	

Spread each half of dough with butter. Combine brown sugar and cinnamon and sprinkle over butter. Roll dough from long side. Cut into 1-1/2 inch slices. Place rolls in greased pans about 3/4 inches apart. Let rise and bake at 350 degrees for 30 minutes. Cool to warm. Makes 2 dozen rolls.

To have grown wise and kind
is real success.

−Anonymous

Cinnamon Flop

Donna Dye
Ray, OH

A favorite recipe found in an old Amish cookbook.

1 c. sugar
2 c. all-purpose flour
2 t. baking powder
1 T. butter, melted

1 c. milk
1/4 c. brown sugar, packed
1 t. cinnamon
1/4 c. butter, sliced

Sift sugar, flour and baking powder together. Add butter and milk and stir until well blended. Divide mixture between 2 well-oiled 9" pie or cake pans. Sprinkle dough with desired amounts of brown sugar and cinnamon, and add pats of butter. Bake at 350 degrees for 30 minutes. Cut into wedges and serve. Makes 8 to 10 servings.

When I was a little girl, I always wanted to be in the kitchen, because it was warm, and that's where my mother was. You never lose that feeling.

– Dolly Parton

Flaky Date Scones

*The Governor's Inn
Ludlow, VT*

Enjoy these topped with homemade preserves or sweet cream butter.

1-1/4 c. all-purpose flour
2-1/2 t. baking powder
1/2 t. salt
2 T. sugar, divided

6 T. butter
2 eggs, beaten
1/3 c. milk
1/2 c. pitted dates, chopped

Mix flour, baking powder, salt, one tablespoon sugar and butter until mixture resembles crumbs. Beat eggs and reserve one tablespoonful. Add milk, dates and eggs to flour mixture; stir until dough is formed. Roll dough on lightly floured surface into 9-inch by 6-inch rectangle, about 1/2-inch thick. Cut into 3-inch squares and then into triangles. Place these about an inch apart on a greased baking sheet. Brush with reserved egg and sprinkle with remaining sugar. Bake at 350 degrees for 12 minutes until golden. Makes one dozen.

Egg cups from the 1950s make delicate vases for springtime tulips or daffodils.

Sugar-Nut Coffee Cake

Eleanor Bierley
Miamisburg, OH

This coffee cake is filled with sweet layers of sugar and nuts! Drizzle with powdered sugar icing, if desired.

3 eggs, beaten
1/2 c. margarine
3/4 c. sugar
1 T. vanilla extract

2 c. all-purpose flour
1 t. baking powder
1 c. sour cream

Lightly oil a Bundt® pan; set aside. In a medium bowl, blend together eggs and margarine. Blend in sugar and vanilla. Sift together flour and baking powder; add to egg mixture. Fold in sour cream. Set aside to prepare sugar-nut mixture.

Sugar-Nut Mixture:

1 c. brown sugar, packed
1 c. chopped nuts

6 T. butter
2 t. cinnamon

Combine all ingredients in a small bowl. Spread half the batter in Bundt® pan; sprinkle sugar-nut mixture evenly over top. Spoon on the remaining batter and gently spread to cover filling. Bake at 350 degrees for 30 minutes. Makes 10 servings.

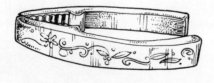

It isn't so much what's on the table that matters,
as what's on the chairs.

–W. S. Gilbert

Farmhouse Breakfasts

Blueberry Coffee Cake

Susan Kennedy
Delaware, OH

A very moist coffee cake, bursting with fresh berry flavor!

2 c. all-purpose flour	1/3 c. margarine, softened
1 c. sugar	1 c. milk
3 t. baking powder	1 egg, beaten
1 t. salt	1 c. blueberries

Beat all ingredients, except blueberries, in a large bowl with an electric mixer on low speed for 30 seconds. Then beat on a medium speed for 2 minutes, scraping bowl occasionally. Grease a 13"x9" baking pan. Spread half the batter in the pan. Sprinkle blueberries over batter, then top with the rest of batter. Add streusel topping; bake at 350 degrees for 40 minutes. Serves 12 to 15.

Streusel:

1/2 c. chopped walnuts	1/2 t. cinnamon
1/3 c. brown sugar, packed	3 t. margarine
1/4 c. all-purpose flour	

Mix all ingredients together until crumbly. Sprinkle on top of coffee cake.

Glaze:

1 c. powdered sugar
2 T. milk
1/4 t. vanilla extract

Combine all ingredients; drizzle over coffee cake.

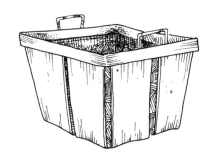

Apple-Stuffed French Toast

Marie Stutz
Denver, PA

It's long been a family tradition that on Sundays, our family attends church services together and then comes home to a yummy brunch. Since we love to eat breakfast, but have little time for it during the week, we make our Sunday gatherings an event. This is one of our favorites.

3 apples, peeled, cored and cut
   into chunks
1/4 c. brown sugar, packed
cinnamon to taste
2 eggs, beaten

1/2 c. milk
1 t. vanilla extract
8 slices wheat bread
Garnish: maple syrup

In a saucepan, combine apples, brown sugar, cinnamon and a small amount of water. Cover and simmer over medium-low heat for 5 to 10 minutes, until apples are soft; set aside. Meanwhile, in a separate bowl, whisk together eggs, milk and vanilla. Heat a greased cast-iron skillet over medium heat. Quickly dip bread into egg mixture, coating both sides; place in skillet. Cook until golden on both sides. To serve, place one slice of French toast on a plate; top with a scoop of apple mixture and another slice of French toast. Drizzle with maple syrup. Makes 4 servings.

Wrap a small twig wreath around homespun napkins!

Coffee Mug Bread

Vickie
Gooseberry Patch

This will be a new favorite!

1 T. cinnamon	1 loaf frozen bread dough
1/2 c. sugar	Garnish: cinnamon sticks
2 T. chopped walnuts	

In a medium bowl, combine cinnamon, sugar and walnuts. Oil the insides of 2 oven-safe coffee mugs. Partially thaw a loaf of frozen bread dough. Cut the loaf in half crosswise. Then divide each half into 4 strips. Roll each strip between the palms of your hands, and then dredge it in cinnamon mixture. Twist 2 strips together, divide in half, and place each half in a spiral fashion into 2 mugs. Repeat with remaining dough. Let the dough rise until double in bulk. The dough will extend beyond the top of the mug and resemble a swirl of whipped cream topping. Bake at 350 degrees for about 15 minutes. Garnish with a cinnamon stick, and serve immediately in the mug. Serves 8.

Animal crackers and cocoa to drink.
That is the finest of suppers, I think.
When I'm grown up and can have
what I please, I think I shall always
insist upon these.

– Christopher Morley

Country Cheese Omelet

Helen Murray
Piketon, OH

Make this a hearty country breakfast and serve with
hashbrowns, biscuits and sausage!

3 eggs, room temperature
1 T. milk
1/4 t. salt
1/4 t. pepper

1 T. butter
1/4 c. finely shredded
 Cheddar cheese

In a medium bowl, whisk together eggs, milk, salt and pepper. In an
8" skillet or omelet pan, melt butter over low heat until foamy but not
browned. Increase the heat to medium-high and tip the pan to coat
with butter. Pour in egg mixture. As the omelet cooks, tilt the pan and
draw the edges in toward the center with a fork. Shake pan gently to
distribute the uncooked portion. When the omelet is just set, about
2 minutes, remove from heat and sprinkle with cheese. Loosen the
edges of the omelet with a fork. As you tip the pan forward to fold the
omelet in half, slide the omelet onto a warmed serving plate. Makes
one serving.

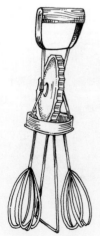

Nothing is quite as intoxicating as the smell of
bacon frying in the morning, save perhaps
the smell of coffee brewing.

–James Beard

Farmhouse Sausage Gravy

Ann Magner
New Port Richey, FL

Create a homestyle breakfast, serve over split buttermilk biscuits!

1/2 lb. mild or sweet ground
   pork sausage
1/2 lb. spicy Italian ground
   pork sausage

3 T. all-purpose flour
3/4 c. milk
3/4 c. chicken broth
salt and pepper to taste

Cook sausage in a large non-stick skillet over medium-high heat until browned. Transfer sausage to a bowl; set aside. Remove all but 3 tablespoons of the fat from the skillet. Sprinkle flour into the skillet; stir well. Cook over medium-high heat for one minute, stirring constantly. Remove skillet from heat and slowly add the milk and the broth. Whisk mixture until completely smooth. Return skillet to the stove and cook until the gravy is slightly thickened. Season with salt and pepper to taste; add the crumbled sausage and combine well. Continue to cook over medium heat until thoroughly heated. Serves 6.

I came from a home
where gravy was
a beverage!

–Erma Bombeck

Rise & Shine Hashbrowns

Sally Foor
Jeromesville, OH

If you want to add a little more flavor to your hashbrowns,
add chopped green pepper and onion to taste.

2 potatoes, peeled
salt and pepper to taste

1 T. oil
1 T. butter

Grate potatoes into a medium bowl and season with salt and pepper. In a non-stick skillet, heat oil and butter over medium heat. Add grated potatoes; pat them down to form a pancake. Cover the skillet and cook potatoes until browned on the bottom. Turn potatoes over and cook 10 minutes longer or until browned. Cut into 4 wedges. Serves 4.

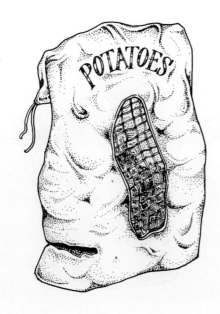

Look for old seed packets at yard sales...they look terrific tucked in cupboard door panels or indoor shutters!

Bacon-Cheddar Cups

Laura Fenneman
Lima, OH

Perfect for a family breakfast buffet...they'll go fast!

12 slices white bread
1 T. butter
4 slices bacon, crisply cooked
  and crumbled
1 egg, beaten
1/2 c. whipping cream

1/2 T. fresh chives, chopped
1/2 T. onion powder
1/2 c. shredded Cheddar cheese
salt and pepper to taste
Garnish: cherry tomatoes,
  mushrooms

Cut a 3-inch circle from center of each slice of bread. Roll out each circle with rolling pin to flatten slightly. Grease a 12-cup muffin tin with butter. Press one bread circle into each cup. Bake at 350 degrees for 7 minutes. Divide bacon among cups. Combine egg, whipping cream, chives and onion powder and divide among cups. Sprinkle with cheese. Bake at 350 degrees for 12 minutes. Let stand 5 minutes before removing to plate. Garnish with cherry tomatoes or mushrooms. Makes one dozen.

Cheese...milk's leap toward immortality.

–Clifton Fadiman

Brown Sugar French Toast

Cherie Shortway
Sussex, NJ

Serve warm from the oven...delicious and so easy!

1 c. brown sugar, packed
1/2 c. butter
2 T. light corn syrup
1 loaf French bread, cut into
    1-inch slices

5 eggs
1-1/2 c. milk
1 t. vanilla extract

Add first 3 ingredients to a medium saucepan and heat over medium heat. Spray a 13"x9" baking pan with non-stick vegetable oil. Pour hot mixture into baking pan. Place sliced bread over mixture and push bread slices closely together. Beat eggs; add milk and vanilla and mix slightly. Pour egg mixture over bread, covering each slice well. Cover the baking pan with plastic wrap and refrigerate overnight. The next morning, uncover and bake at 350 degrees for 30 minutes. Serve directly from baking pan or turn onto plates. Serves 6 to 8.

Oh, it's nice to get up on the mornin', but it's nicer to lie in bed.

–Sir Harry Lauder

Garden-Fresh Denver Omelet

Donna Dye
Ray, OH

You can add any of your favorite vegetables, fresh from the garden!

1 slice bacon, cut into
  1/2-inch pieces
2 T. red pepper, diced
2 T. green pepper, diced
2 T. red onion, diced
1 slice baked ham, shredded

2 eggs, beaten
1/4 c. milk
salt and pepper to taste
1 t. fresh chives, chopped
2 t. butter
Garnish: sour cream and salsa

Cook bacon in a non-stick skillet over medium-low heat until just crisp, 5 minutes. Using a slotted spoon, transfer bacon to a paper towel to drain. Remove and discard all but one tablespoon of bacon fat. Add both peppers and onion to skillet and cook over low heat, stirring until just wilted, about 5 minutes. Transfer the vegetables to a bowl and add bacon and ham. In a separate bowl, beat eggs with milk. Season with salt and pepper and whisk in chives. Stir in vegetable mixture. Melt butter in a non-stick skillet over medium heat until it foams. Add egg mixture and cook without stirring until omelet begins to set around the edges. Using a fork, push the set eggs into the center letting the uncooked eggs run out to edges. Continue cooking, making sure filling is distributed evenly. Cover and cook for 30 to 45 seconds more, or until eggs are cooked to the desired doneness. Slide omelet halfway onto a plate, then flip it over itself. Serve with sour cream and salsa. Makes one serving.

Love and eggs are best when they are fresh.

– Russian saying

Early Riser Home Fries

Becky Sykes
Delaware, OH

Serve these crispy potatoes with eggs and sausage on the side!

4 russet potatoes
1/4 c. oil
1 green pepper, chopped

1 onion, chopped
salt and pepper to taste

Pierce potatoes with the tines of a fork. Bake potatoes at 375 degrees
for one hour. When potatoes have cooled slightly, cut them into
one-inch cubes. Heat oil in a large non-stick skillet over medium heat
and add green pepper and onion. Cook until lightly browned, about
10 minutes. Add potatoes to skillet and stir well. Add salt and pepper
to taste. Continue to cook potatoes for 10 minutes, or until crispy and
lightly browned, turning occasionally with a spatula. Serves 4 to 6.

Nothing helps scenery like ham and eggs.

– Mark Twain

Old-fashioned Breads

As kids, we always came home through the kitchen door. Just outside was a woodpile stacked high, kindling in a brass bucket and the scent of woodsmoke in the air. We'd stop just long enough to take off muddy boots or wet shoes, Mom's rule, and then run inside! It was our favorite place because Mom could be found there.

One of our best memories is the aroma of bread baking in the oven...we could hardly wait to have some, still warm with lots of butter! We'd sink our teeth into a thick slice, gobble it up and ask for another! Sometimes we topped it with homemade jam and we always had a glass of icy cold milk.

Even today, the smell of freshly baked bread takes me back to those days.

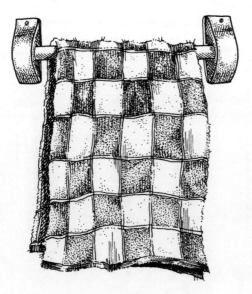

Old-fashioned Breads

The Best Bread in the World

Ann Marie Pastore
Powell, OH

Very easy to make and such a treat when the butter melts instantly on a still-warm slice.

2 c. boiling water
1 c. rolled oats, uncooked
1/3 c. lukewarm water
2 pkgs. active dry yeast
1 T. salt
1/2 c. honey

2 T. butter, melted and cooled
2-1/2 to 3 c. unbleached flour
1-1/2 to 2 c. whole-wheat flour
1 egg yolk
1 T. water
sesame seed to taste

Pour water over oats. Let stand until thoroughly softened, adding additional boiling water if necessary. In another bowl, soak yeast in lukewarm water. Add salt, honey and melted butter to oat mixture. Making sure the oats are lukewarm, add yeast mixture and mix well. Gradually add flours and knead with your hands, about 5 minutes. Put dough into a lightly oiled bowl, turning it around to coat dough on all sides. Cover with a cloth and let rise for one hour or until doubled. Oil, or spray 2, 9"x5" loaf pans or baking sheets. Punch down the risen bread dough and cut in half. Knead each half briefly and shape into loaves. Place loaves in pans. Beat egg yolk with water and brush surface of each loaf; sprinkle with sesame seed. Bake at 350 degrees for 35 to 40 minutes. Turn the loaves onto a rack and let cool. Makes 2 loaves.

Use your summer herbs to make beautiful wreaths. Sage and Sweet Annie are long-lasting and fragrant!

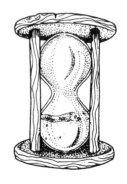

Sour Cream Corn Muffins

Kathy Moberg
Saline, MI

Serve warm with a bowl of chili or vegetable soup.

1 c. yellow cornmeal
1 c. all-purpose flour
1/4 c. sugar
2 t. baking powder
1/2 t. baking soda

1 t. salt
1 c. sour cream
2 eggs, beaten
1/4 c. butter, melted

In a large bowl, combine cornmeal, flour, sugar, baking powder, baking soda and salt. Mix together. In a small bowl, combine sour cream, eggs and butter. Mix thoroughly; add to dry ingredients. Stir until moistened. Spoon batter into a well-greased muffin tin. Bake at 425 degrees for 15 to 20 minutes, until golden. Makes one dozen.

Honest bread is very well...
it's the butter that makes
the temptation.

– Douglas William Jerrold

Old-fashioned Breads

Featherbed Rolls

Liz Kenneweg
Butler, OH

This recipe comes from a very old family cookbook my mother had...
it's listed under the section, "Foods Men Rave About!"

1 cake compressed yeast
2-1/2 c. milk
1/2 c. shortening
2 T. sugar

2 t. salt
5 c. all-purpose flour
Garnish: melted butter

Crumble yeast into a bowl. Heat milk to boiling; cool to 80 degrees. Add to yeast. Blend shortening and sugar together. Add salt and yeast mixture. Sift flour once before measuring. Add flour to yeast mixture and beat with a spoon until smooth. Allow to rise until double in bulk, about one hour. Place a spoonful of dough into each greased muffin cup, filling 2/3 full. Let rise again until double in bulk, 20 to 30 minutes. Bake at 425 degrees for 20 minutes or until golden brown. Brush rolls with butter after removing them from the oven. Makes 3 dozen rolls.

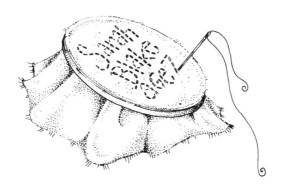

Jelly is a food usually found on bread,
children and piano keys.

– Anonymous

Grandma's Special Potato Buns

Shirley Young
Jersey Shore, PA

This recipe brings back wonderful childhood memories of going to Grandma's house. As soon as we walked into her old farmhouse, we'd head for the out-kitchen to sample her bounty.

1 pkg. active dry yeast
1 c. lukewarm water
1 c. mashed potatoes
2 eggs, beaten
1/2 c. shortening

1/2 c. sugar
1 t. salt
3-1/2 c. all-purpose flour
Garnish: melted butter, sugar

Dissolve yeast in lukewarmwater. Combine with potatoes, eggs, shortening, sugar and salt. Mix well. Blend in flour. Place dough in an oiled bowl, turning once to coat. Let dough rise for 2 hours. Roll out to 1/2-inch thick and cut with a biscuit cutter. Arrange on a lightly greased baking sheet. Let rise. Rub butter on tops and sprinkle lightly with sugar. Bake at 400 degrees for 7 minutes or until tops begin to brown. Makes 1-1/2 to 2 dozen.

Bread is like dresses, hats and shoes...
in other words, essential!

– Emily Post

Old-fashioned Breads

Poppy Seed Bread

Linda Thomas
Everett, WA

An old-fashioned sweet bread.

3 eggs
1-1/2 c. milk
1-1/8 c. oil
1-1/2 t. vanilla extract
1-1/2 t. almond extract
1-1/2 t. butter flavoring

2-1/3 c. sugar
2 T. poppy seed
1-1/2 t. salt
1/2 t. baking powder
3 c. all-purpose flour

Beat eggs together in a large bowl. Add milk, oil and extracts; mix well. Add remaining ingredients. Pour batter into 2 lightly greased 9"x5" loaf pans and bake at 325 degrees for one hour. Let cool for 10 minutes in pans. Pour Glaze on top and leave in pans to cool completely. Makes 2 loaves.

Glaze:

1/2 c. sugar
1/4 c. orange juice
1/2 t. vanilla extract

1/2 t. almond extract
1/2 t. butter flavoring

Mix all ingredients together until sugar is dissolved completely.

*What is a home
without Mother?*

–Alice Hawthorne

Apple-Nut Bread

Angie Stevens
South Point, OH

*Serve this bread with an icy cold glass of milk...it makes
a yummy after-school treat!*

2 c. oil
1-1/2 c. sugar
3 eggs, beaten
1 t. vanilla extract
3 c. all-purpose flour
1-1/2 t. baking soda
1/2 t. salt

1 t. cinnamon
1 t. nutmeg
1 t. ground cloves
1 t. ground ginger
3 c. apples, cored and chopped
1 c. chopped nuts

Combine oil, sugar, eggs and vanilla in a mixing bowl; beat with an
electric mixer on low speed until blended. In a separate bowl, mix
together flour, baking soda, salt and spices. Add to oil mixture. Beat
on low speed until blended. Stir in apples and nuts and mix well by
hand. Pour batter into a greased and floured Bundt® pan. Bake at
350 degrees for one hour and 15 minutes. Let cool in pan for
15 minutes before removing. Serves 10 to 12.

*A child-size coffeepot is the perfect place to display
your favorite coffee-scented candles!*

Loving Loaf

Sandy White
Long Beach, MS

An "upside-down" loaf of bread!

Topping:

1/2 c. butter, melted
1/3 c. sugar

1-1/2 c. vanilla wafers, crushed
1 c. pecans, finely chopped

Combine topping ingredients. Mix thoroughly. Pat into bottom of 2 well-greased 9"x5" loaf pans. Set aside.

Batter:

1 c. butter
2 c. sugar
4 eggs, beaten
1 c. milk

2 t. vanilla extract
2-2/3 c. all-purpose flour
1-1/2 t. baking powder
1/2 t. salt

Blend butter and sugar together. Add eggs, one at a time and beat well after each one. In a separate bowl, combine milk and vanilla. In another bowl sift flour, baking powder, and salt together. Add to butter mixture, alternately beginning with milk and ending with flour. Beat well. Pour into loaf pans. Bake at 350 degrees for one hour. Cool on wire racks; invert loaves onto serving plate. Makes 2 loaves

The mother's heart is the child's schoolroom.

–Henry Ward Beecher

Buttermilk Biscuits

Vickie
Gooseberry Patch

Serve these warm from the oven with Tin Can Butter
or homemade jam.

2 c. all-purpose flour
1 t. baking soda
1 t. cream of tartar

1/8 t. salt
3 T. shortening
1 c. buttermilk

Cut all ingredients except buttermilk together to make fine crumbs. Add buttermilk, stirring with a fork until soft dough is formed. Roll out dough 1/2-inch thick on a floured surface and cut with biscuit cutter. Arrange on an ungreased baking sheet. Bake at 450 degrees for 10 to 12 minutes or until lightly browned. Makes one dozen biscuits.

Tin Can Butter:

Add whipping cream to a quart or half-gallon can, tighten down the lid and give to your children to roll across the floor! In 15 to 30 minutes you'll have freshly "churned" butter!

The King asked the Queen, and the Queen asked the Dairymaid: "Could we have some butter for the royal slice of bread?"

–A. A. Milne

Cinnamon-Carrot Nut Bread

Pat Habiger
Spearville, KS

A dark, easy-to-make bread that will stay moist for days...
if it lasts that long!

2-1/2 c. carrots, peeled
   and shredded
1 c. pecans, finely chopped
2 c. unbleached flour
1-1/2 c. sugar
2 t. baking powder

2 t. cinnamon
1 t. salt
3 eggs, beaten
1-1/2 c. oil
2 t. vanilla extract

In a medium bowl, toss together carrots and pecans and set aside. In another bowl, stir together flour, sugar, baking powder, cinnamon and salt. Set aside. In a large bowl, beat eggs with an electric mixer on low speed. Beat in oil and vanilla. Gradually beat in flour mixture, then carrot mixture. Turn into a well-greased 10" tube pan. Bake at 325 degrees for one hour and 10 minutes or until a toothpick inserted in center comes out clean. Cool completely. Makes 24 servings.

For a family picnic, fill a granite-enamel pail with crushed ice and lots of ice cream treats!

Blueberry Bread

Gail Prendergast
Lancaster, PA

This recipe has been handed down in my family for many years.
A great sweet and tart bread.

1 c. sugar
3 c. plus 2 t. all-purpose
 flour, divided
1 t. salt
4 t. baking powder

1 egg, beaten
1 c. milk
2 T. butter, melted
juice of 1/2 lemon
1 c. blueberries

Sift together sugar, 3 cups of flour, salt and baking powder in a bowl. Add egg, milk and butter. Mix with a wooden spoon, do not beat. Add lemon juice. Toss blueberries with remaining flour, fold into mixture. Spread in a greased 9"x5" loaf pan and bake at 350 degrees for one hour. Makes one loaf.

A good laugh is sunshine in the house.

–Thackeray

Lemon Clover Rolls

Liz Kenneweg
Butler, OH

This recipe came in a cookbook my mother received from family members when she first got married...it's over 75 years old.

2 c. all-purpose flour
3/4 t. baking soda
1/2 t. salt
1/4 c. plus 2 t. sugar, divided

1/3 c. shortening
1/2 c. milk
3 T. lemon juice

Sift, then measure flour. Sift again with the baking soda, salt and 1/4 cup sugar. Cut shortening into flour mixture until it resembles cornmeal. In a cup, combine milk and lemon juice; add to flour mixture. Stir quickly to form a soft dough. Turn onto a lightly floured board. Knead slightly. Form dough into balls about the size of marbles. Place 3 balls in each lightly oiled muffin tin. Sprinkle with remaining sugar. Bake at 450 degrees for 20 minutes. Makes one dozen rolls.

Cut out heart shapes from worn-out quilts, stuff them, sew closed and stitch an old button on the front. Pile them in an old tin pan or yelloware mixing bowl!

Muffin Pan Rolls

Kathie Stout
Worthington, OH

Easy to make; so delicious with apple butter!

1 pkg. active dry yeast
3/4 c. very warm water,
   110 to 115 degrees
2 c. all-purpose flour, sifted
   and divided

3/4 t. salt
1-1/2 T. sugar
1 egg, beaten
2 T. shortening, melted

Dissolve yeast in warm water; let stand 3 minutes. Add one cup flour, salt, sugar, egg and shortening. Beat until smooth. Add remaining flour and stir until flour is fully blended in. Let rise until double in size, about 30 minutes. Spoon into greased muffin pans. Let rise again for 30 minutes. Bake at 425 degrees for 15 minutes. Makes one dozen.

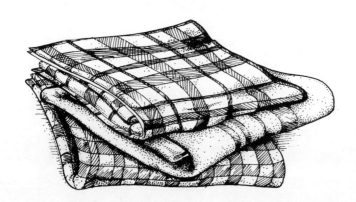

Friends, books, a cheerful heart and a conscience clear
are the most choice companions we have here.

– William Mather

Old-fashioned Breads

Aunt Hazel's French Bread

Dar Stuart
Battle Ground, WA

*A recipe I have made for many years; it's easy
and excellent every time!*

2 c. boiling water
1/4 c. plus 1 t. honey, divided
2 T. oil
2 t. salt

2 T. active dry yeast
1/2 c. warm water
6 to 8 c. all-purpose flour
Garnish: melted butter

Mix boiling water, 1/4 cup honey, oil and salt together and let cool in mixing bowl. In a separate bowl add yeast, warm water and remaining honey. Mix and set aside for 10 minutes. Add yeast mixture to water mixture. Add flour until dough is no longer sticky, between 6 to 8 cups. Using a dough hook in a heavy-duty electric mixer, beat the dough for 10 minutes, 5 times. On 6th time, turn out on floured board and shape into 2 loaves. Place in 2 greased 9"x5" loaf pans. Let rise 30 minutes, then slice the top diagonally. Bake at 400 degrees for 20 minutes. Remove bread from oven and brush top with butter while still hot. Makes 2 loaves.

An old-fashioned wooden ladder that's been attached to hooks in your kitchen ceiling is the perfect place to display your basket collection...tie the baskets on with several strands of raffia.

Cinnamon Streusel Quick Bread

Jana Warnell
Kalispell, MT

As a newlywed, the best compliments are always from my husband. He really loves this bread and I love making it for him, so it's never long before I have to make another loaf!

2 c. all-purpose flour
4 t. baking powder
1-1/4 t. salt
1/3 c. oil
2 eggs, beaten

1 c. sugar
1-1/2 t. cinnamon
1 c. buttermilk
2 t. vanilla extract

Grease and flour bottom only of one 9"x5" pan or 2, 8"x4" loaf pans. Combine all ingredients and beat 3 minutes with an electric mixer on medium speed. Pour half the batter into the prepared pans. Sprinkle Streusel over batter. Pour the rest of the batter over the streusel. (You can make extra streusel for the top.) Bake at 350 degrees for 45 to 55 minutes. Remove from pans immediately and cool on wire racks. Makes 2 loaves.

Streusel:

1/2 c. brown sugar
1 t. cinnamon

2 T. butter, softened

Combine all ingredients and mix well.

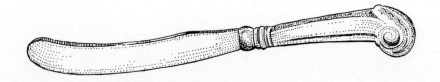

The best antique is an old friend.

– Anonymous

Corn Spoon Bread

Crystal Lappie
Worthington, OH

*An old-fashioned favorite. My husband and I enjoy it with
a hot bowl of chili or home-style beef stew.*

1/2 c. butter
15-1/4 oz. can whole-kernel
  corn, drained

14-3/4 oz. can cream-style corn
8-1/2 oz. pkg. corn muffin mix
1 c. sour cream

Preheat oven to 350 degrees. Place butter in a 12"x7" baking pan,
place pan in oven until butter melts. Add remaining ingredients to
baking pan and mix well. Bake at 350 degrees for 25 to 30 minutes
or until golden. Cut into squares. Makes 6 to 8 servings.

Bachelor's fare: bread and cheese and kisses.

–Jonathan Swift

Grandmother's Rolls

Sally Foor
Jeromesville, OH

Make these rolls a family tradition in your home.
They're golden and so delicious!

1 c. shortening
3/4 c. sugar
2 t. salt
1 c. boiling water
2 pkgs. active dry yeast
1/2 c. very warm water,
    110 to 115 degrees

3 eggs
7-1/2 c. all-purpose flour
1 c. cold water
1 T. oil

Blend shortening, sugar and salt. Add boiling water. Stir until smooth. Dissolve yeast in warm water. Beat eggs; add to yeast mixture. Cool shortening mixture slightly; add yeast and egg mixture. Add flour alternately with cold water. Stir until dough is smooth. Lightly oil the top and cover tightly with wax paper. Put a piece of aluminum foil over the paper, securing tightly. Place in refrigerator overnight. Remove dough from refrigerator 3 hours before baking. Punch dough down and let rest 5 minutes. Shape into walnut-sized balls; add 3 balls per cup to a lightly oiled muffin pan. Let formed rolls rest in a warm place until they fill the pans. Bake at 400 degrees for 12 minutes. Makes 4 dozen cloverleaf rolls.

Grandma's old candle box looks wonderful filled with your favorite potpourri and a pillar candle!

Old-fashioned Breads

Country Inn Soda Bread
Abel Darling Bed & Breakfast
Litchfield, CT

Many of our guests have gone home with this recipe;
it's always a favorite at the inn.

3 c. all-purpose flour
1/2 c. dark raisins
1/2 c. golden raisins
1/2 c. currants
2 t. baking powder

1 t. salt
1/2 c. sugar
1-1/2 c. buttermilk
3 t. caraway seed

In a large bowl combine all ingredients together; mix thoroughly.
Oil a cast-iron skillet; add dough to skillet. Bake at 350 degrees for
45 minutes. Makes one loaf.

I never had a piece of toast,
particularly long and wide, but
fell upon the sanded floor, and
always on the buttered side.

– James Payne

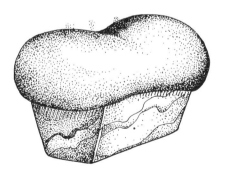

Mile-High Biscuits

Gail Banasiak
Dayton, OH

A golden biscuit, perfect served with honey-butter. For an easy breakfast, make them the night before and refrigerate biscuits on your baking sheet until morning.

2 c. all-purpose flour
4 t. baking powder
1 T. sugar
1/2 t. salt

1/2 c. shortening
1 egg, beaten
2/3 c. milk

Sift together flour, baking powder, sugar and salt into a large bowl. Cut in shortening with a pastry cutter until mixture resembles coarse crumbs. Combine egg and milk with a whisk, then add all at once to flour mixture. Stir with a fork only until dough follows it around bowl. Turn dough out onto a lightly floured board. Knead very gently with the heels of your hands about 5 to 7 times. Dough will be very moist. Pat or roll out dough to 3/4-inch thickness. Cut into 2-inch squares. Place on an ungreased baking sheet, one inch apart. You can now refrigerate the biscuits until ready to bake, or bake at 450 degrees for 10 to 12 minutes or until golden. Makes one dozen.

A cobalt blue pitcher adds beautiful color to your kitchen! Fill it with kitchen utensils or a bright yellow sunflower!

Country Kitchen Potato Bread

Kathie Stout
Worthington, OH

A wonderful old recipe. Perfect every time!

1 large potato, peeled and diced	3 eggs, beaten
1 c. cold water	2 pkgs. active dry yeast
1 t. salt	1/4 c. very warm water,
1/2 c. butter	110-115 degrees
1/2 c. sugar	6 c. all-purpose flour
1/2 c. powdered milk	

Combine potato, cold water and salt in a large saucepan. Boil, covered, until potato is tender. Remove from heat, but do not drain. Add butter and sugar; beat with an electric mixer until smooth. Beat in powdered milk and eggs. Dissolve yeast in warm water and add to mixture. With a wooden spoon, beat in enough flour to make a soft dough, about 4 cups. Work in remaining flour until smooth, turning out onto a floured board if necessary. Place dough in a generously buttered large bowl, turning it over so top is greased. Cover with a damp towel and set in a warm place. Let rise until doubled, about 1-1/2 hours. Punch down; cover and refrigerate overnight. The next day, let rise at room temperature for several hours. Divide dough into 2, 9"x5" buttered loaf pans. Cover and let rise again until doubled, about one hour. Bake at 375 degrees for 35 to 40 minutes. Set on wire racks to cool. Makes 2 loaves.

Babies are such a nice way to start people.

– Don Herold

Sweet Potato Biscuits

Kathy Jo Croom
Bailey, CO

A family favorite in our home and a great take-along snack for traveling.

29-oz. can yams, drained and
   mashed
1/2 c. butter, softened
1/2 c. sugar
2 T. milk

1 t. salt
3-1/2 to 4 c. all-purpose flour
4-1/2 t. baking powder
cinnamon to taste

Combine yams, butter, sugar, milk and salt. Mix thoroughly. In another bowl, sift flour, baking powder and cinnamon together. Add to yam mixture. Mix with hands to form a soft dough, adding more flour if needed. On a floured surface, roll dough to one-inch thickness. Cut with cookie cutter and place on greased baking sheet. Bake at 350 degrees for 15 to 20 minutes or until light golden brown. Makes 2 dozen.

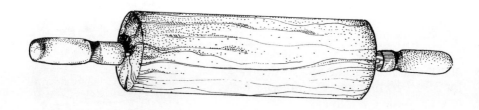

Bread is the warmest, kindest of words. Write it always with a capital letter, like your own name.

– Russian Café Sign

Old-fashioned Breads

Corn Fritters

Barbara Arnold
Toledo, OH

Wonderful served with fresh butter and maple syrup.

1-1/2 c. all-purpose flour
14-1/2 oz. can cream-style corn
1 egg, beaten

2 T. sugar
1 T. baking powder
oil for frying

In a bowl, combine all ingredients, except oil. In a large skillet, pour oil to a depth of 1/2 inch and heat. Drop batter from rounded tablespoons into hot oil. Fry 2 minutes on each side or until golden brown. Remove from skillet and drain on paper towels. Serves 6.

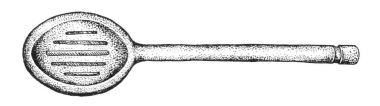

English Muffins

Donna Dye
Ray, OH

I like to add cranberries to the mix.

1 pkg. active dry yeast
1-1/2 c. very warm water,
    110 to 115 degrees
3 T. sugar
1/2 c. powdered milk

1 t. salt
1 egg, beaten
3 T. butter
4 c. all-purpose flour
small amounts oil, cornmeal

Dissolve yeast in warm water. Add next 5 ingredients; blend in flour. Let rise until double in bulk. Punch down and shape muffins, flattening slightly. Oil griddle surface and lightly scatter with cornmeal. Cook muffins as you would pancakes, turning when golden. Makes 6 to 8 muffins.

Garlic Pull-Aparts

Liz Plotnick-Snay
Gooseberry Patch

So easy to make! Serve warm with herb butter.

1 loaf frozen whole-wheat or
  white bread dough, thawed,
  cut into 32 pieces
1/3 c. butter, melted

2 T. fresh parsley, chopped
2 T. onion, finely chopped
1 t. fresh garlic, finely chopped
1/4 t. salt

Place bread dough in a large bowl. In a smaller bowl, combine remaining ingredients. Pour over bread dough. Toss to coat well. Arrange bread dough in a greased 1-1/2 quart casserole dish or 1-1/2 quart soufflé pan. Cover and let rise in warm place until double in size. Bake at 375 degrees for 30 to 35 minutes or until golden brown. If bread begins to brown too quickly, shield with aluminum foil. Cool 10 minutes. Invert pan to remove bread. Serve warm. Serves 8.

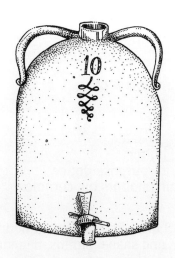

Attach pegs to the long side
of an old-fashioned gameboard...
a wonderful peg rack to display
bundles of your favorite herbs!

Simmering
Soups

On a cool autumn day, we'd gather together as a family and drive until we found a farmstand. Cornstalks surrounded the fence posts, Indian corn was swinging from the beams and baskets were overflowing with gourds, apples and pumpkins! Everywhere we looked there were crates of eggs, jugs of freshly-pressed cider, and heaps of potatoes for sale!

The most exciting thing for the kids, however, was picking pumpkins! We'd always need one that was just ours, and Mom needed a few small ones for the porch, windowsills and steps...the ride home was always a little crowded!

After arriving home, we'd find just the right place for each pumpkin, while Mom prepared a hearty stew or chowder to warm us up. It always required slow simmering and made the house smell so nice. When it was done, she'd call us inside. We'd peel off jackets and sweaters and sit down to homemade soup served in thick white bowls... perfect on such a clear, crisp day!

Simmering Soups

Country Chicken Stew

Kay Marone
Des Moines, IA

A savory, filling meal in a bowl.

4 boneless, skinless chicken
    thighs
3-1/2 c. chicken broth
2 c. plum tomatoes, chopped
1 c. green pepper, chopped
1 c. onion, chopped
1/2 c. long-cooking rice,
    uncooked

1/2 c. canned garbanzo beans,
    drained and rinsed
3 cloves garlic, chopped
1/2 t. salt
1/2 t. pepper
1 bay leaf
Garnish: shredded Monterey
    Jack cheese, diced avocado

Combine all ingredients except garnish in a slow cooker. Cover and cook on low setting for 7 to 9 hours, until chicken and rice are tender. Discard bay leaf. To serve, place a chicken thigh in each soup bowl; top with soup and garnish as desired. Makes 4 servings.

Good manners: The noise you don't make
when you're eating soup.

– Bennett Cerf

Broccoli Cheddar Soup

Donna Nowicki
Center City, MN

We serve this creamy soup with warm, crusty bread. It's a hearty, complete meal and so comforting on a crisp evening.

3/4 c. onion, finely chopped
3/4 c. butter
3/4 c. all-purpose flour
1 t. salt
1 t. pepper

3 c. chicken broth
4-1/2 c. milk
3 c. fresh broccoli, chopped
and cooked
3/4 c. shredded Cheddar cheese

In a saucepan, sauté the onion in butter until tender. Stir in flour, salt and pepper. Cook and stir until smooth and bubbly. Add broth and milk all at once. Cook and stir until the mixture boils and thickens. Add broccoli. Simmer, stirring constantly, until heated through. Remove from heat. Stir in cheese until melted. Serves 6.

Do not wish for any other blessing than a good wife and rich soup.

– Russian proverb

Simmering Soups

Farmstead Split Pea Soup

Jo Ann
Gooseberry Patch

Fill a thermos with this hearty soup...terrific for an autumn picnic.

8 c. water
1-lb. bag split peas, rinsed
   and drained
1 ham bone with meat
2 onions, chopped
3 leeks, white part only, chopped
2 stalks celery, chopped

1 carrot, peeled and chopped
1 c. dry white wine
1 clove garlic, finely chopped
1/2 t.dried marjoram
1/4 t. dried thyme
salt and pepper to taste

In a Dutch oven, combine all ingredients except salt and pepper. Bring to a boil. Reduce heat to low, cover and simmer for 2 to 2-1/2 hours or until peas are soft. Remove ham bone and cool to warm. Remove meat from bone and add meat to Dutch oven. Add salt and pepper to taste. Serves 6.

A stack of stools is a wonderful way to display children's alphabet blocks, old-fashioned toys, Shaker boxes, candles, or filled apothecary jars.

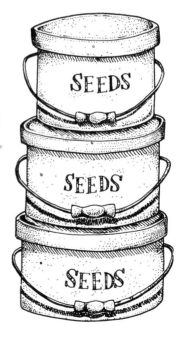

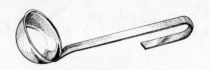

Grandma's Chili

Cheryl Waite
DeKalb, IL

This recipe was passed down from my grandmother to my mother, who passed it on to me. The bacon gives it a special flavor!

4 slices bacon, diced	1 t. salt
1-1/2 lbs. ground beef	1 clove garlic, minced
1 onion, chopped	1 T. chili powder
1/2 c. green pepper, chopped	16-oz. can tomato sauce
3 tomatoes, chopped	2 16-oz. cans kidney beans,
2 t. sugar	drained

In a medium skillet, fry bacon until crisp. Remove from skillet and drain on paper towels. Add ground beef and cook thoroughly. Add remaining ingredients except beans; simmer for one hour. Add beans and cook an additional 20 minutes. You can also prepare this chili in your slow cooker; cook on low setting for 6 to 8 hours. Serves 6 to 8.

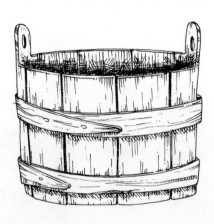

Set children's blocks, old-fashioned school books or a child's lunch bucket on your old schoolhouse chair.

Norwegian Soup Au Gratin

Eleanor Bierley
Miamisburg, OH

A family wintertime tradition! We love to get together to share this warm soup and memories on a cold winter night.

3 T. butter
1/4 lb. hard salami, sliced and
  chopped into 1/2-inch pieces
1/2 c. carrot, peeled and
  thinly sliced
1/3 c. green onions, chopped
1 clove garlic, minced
2-1/2 c. water
1 c. cabbage, shredded

2 T. orzo pasta, uncooked
2 t. chicken bouillon granules
1/4 t. pepper
1 T. dried parsley
1/2 c. whipping cream
8 slices French bread
3/4 c. shredded Swiss or
  mozzarella cheese

In a large saucepan, melt butter. Sauté salami, carrot, onions and garlic for 5 minutes. Add water, cabbage, macaroni, chicken bouillon, and pepper. Reduce heat. Cover and simmer 12 minutes. Add parsley. Continue to simmer an additional 3 minutes. Stir in cream. Pour equally into 4, 10-ounce soup crocks; set on a baking sheet. Top each with 2 slices French bread, side by side. Sprinkle equally with shredded cheese. Broil 3 to 5 minutes, until cheese melts and becomes golden. Serves 4.

Happiness often sneaks in through a door you didn't know you left open.

–John Barrymore

Tomato Bisque

Sandy Spayer
Jeromesville, OH

An old-fashioned favorite! Perfect with a grilled cheese sandwich.

2 c. chicken broth
14-1/2 oz. can whole tomatoes,
   broken up
1/2 c. celery, chopped
1/2 c. onion, chopped

3 tomatoes, chopped
3 T. butter
3 T. all-purpose flour
2 c. half-and-half
1 T. sugar

In a large saucepan over medium heat, combine broth, canned tomatoes with juice, celery and onion; bring to a boil. Reduce heat; cover and simmer for 20 minutes. In a blender or food processor, process mixture in small batches until smooth. In the same saucepan, cook chopped tomatoes in butter for about 5 minutes; stir in flour. Add half-and-half; cook and stir over low heat until thickened. Stir in processed broth mixture and sugar; heat through without boiling. Makes 6 servings.

Old wooden storage boxes look great with the drawers slightly open. Fill them with dried orange slices, pepperberries, herbs or potpourri.

Simmering Soups

Onion Soup

Mary Murray
Mt. Vernon, OH

One of our favorites! Try sweet Vidalia onions for a sweeter taste.

2 T. butter
5 yellow onions, thinly sliced
2 T. sugar
3-1/2 c. beef broth
5 c. water

1/2 t. salt
1/2 t. pepper
4 slices French bread, toasted
4 T. Gruyère cheese, shredded

In a 5-quart Dutch oven, melt butter over medium-high heat. Add onions and sugar. Sauté until onions are lightly golden, about 10 minutes. Reduce heat to low and sauté 10 more minutes, stirring often. Add broth and water; bring to a boil over high heat. Reduce heat to simmer and cook, uncovered, for 20 minutes. Add salt and pepper to taste, bring just to boiling over high heat. Ladle soup into 4, 8-ounce oven proof soup bowls; place bowls on a baking sheet. Top each bowl with a slice of toasted French bread and sprinkle with one tablespoon cheese. Bake, uncovered, at 400 degrees until cheese is melted, about 5 minutes. Serves 4.

It is probably illegal to make soups, stews and casseroles without plenty of onions.

– Maggie Waldron

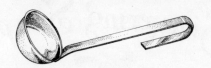

Barley Vegetable Soup

Karen Urfer
New Philadelphia, OH

A great soup our family enjoys after raking leaves or
a winter snowball fight!

1/2 lb. ground turkey
1/2 c. onion, chopped
1 clove garlic, pressed
7 c. water
28-oz. can stewed tomatoes
1/2 c. pearled barley, uncooked
1/2 c. celery, sliced

1/2 c. carrot, sliced
2 beef bouillon cubes
1/2 t. dried basil
1 bay leaf
salt and pepper to taste
9-oz. pkg. frozen mixed
    vegetables

In a Dutch oven, brown turkey. Add onion and garlic; cook until tender. Stir in water, tomatoes with juice and remaining ingredients except frozen vegetables. Cover and bring to a boil. Reduce heat and simmer for one hour. Add frozen vegetables and cook an additional 15 minutes. Add additional water if needed. Discard bay leaf and serve. Makes 4 servings.

Only the pure in heart can make good soup.

– Beethoven

Broccoli Cheese Noodle Soup
Debbie Cummons-Parker
Lakeview, OH

A creamy soup that's really filling.

3/4 c. onion, chopped
2 T. oil
6 c. boiling water
6 chicken bouillon cubes
8-oz. pkg. egg noodles,
   uncooked
20-oz. pkg. frozen chopped
   broccoli

1 lb. pasteurized process
   cheese, cubed
6 c. milk
1 t. salt
pepper and garlic powder
   to taste

Sauté onion in oil; set aside. To the boiling water, add bouillon cubes, noodles and broccoli. Cook until tender. Add onion, cheese, milk, salt, pepper and garlic powder. Cover and simmer until heated through and cheese is melted. Soup can be made ahead and frozen. To reheat, either use a double boiler or microwave, as it scorches easily. Serves 16.

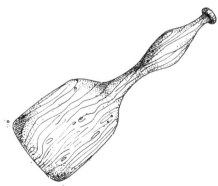

Laughter is the brush that sweeps away
the cobwebs of the heart.

– Mort Walker

Chicken Mulligan

Judy Kelly
St. Charles, MO

I first served this at a casual New Year's Eve party...it can be made ahead of time and simply reheated before guests arrive.

2 to 3 whole chickens, cut up
4 16-oz. cans pork & beans
16-oz. can whole tomatoes, chopped
16-oz. can corn, drained
2 16-oz cans lima beans
1 lb. cabbage, shredded
1 lb. carrots, sliced

1 bunch celery, chopped
46-oz. can vegetable juice cocktail
14-oz. bottle catsup
1 onion, chopped
2 lbs. potatoes, peeled and diced
salt and pepper to taste

Remove skin from chicken pieces; arrange chicken in a roasting pan. Bake, covered, at 375 degrees for one hour. Reserve the drippings in a bowl; cool and skim surface. Remove the meat from the bones; cut into one-inch pieces. Combine the skimmed drippings and chicken in a 3-gallon stockpot. Add remaining ingredients. Simmer for 1-1/2 hours, stirring frequently. Serves 20.

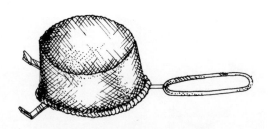

A new baby is like the beginning of all things...wonder, hope, a dream of possibilities.

– Eda J. Le Shan

Simmering Soups

Old-Fashioned Beef Stew

Linda Romano
Canonsburg, PA

I love to dip Italian bread in this soup!

2 T. oil
3 cloves garlic, minced
1-1/2 lbs. stew beef cubes
2 c. water
1/2 c. tomato sauce or juice
1 bay leaf

salt and pepper to taste
3 potatoes, peeled and cubed
2 carrots, peeled and diced
2 c. frozen green beans
2 T. French onion soup mix
1 to 2 T. flour

In a Dutch oven, sauté oil, garlic and beef until browned. Add water, tomato sauce or juice and bay leaf; season with salt and pepper to taste. Cover and let simmer for an hour. After one hour, add potatoes, carrots and green beans. Sprinkle with French onion soup mix. Cook for 30 minutes, or until all is tender. Discard bay leaf. Add flour as needed to thicken. Serves 4 to 6.

Don't be afraid to take big steps. You can't cross a chasm in two small jumps.

– David L. George

Cheesy Potato Soup

Kim Roepke
Omaha, NE

A big bowl of this creamy soup is perfect comfort food.

1/2 c. carrot, peeled and chopped
1/4 c. onion, chopped
1/2 c. celery, chopped
3 c. potatoes, peeled and diced
1 c. water
1 t. dried parsley
1/2 t. salt

1/8 t. pepper
1 chicken bouillon cube
2 T. all-purpose flour
1-1/2 c. milk
1/2 lb. pasteurized process
    cheese, cubed

In a soup pot, combine vegetables, water, seasonings and bouillon cube. Simmer until vegetables are tender. Blend together flour and milk in a separate bowl. Add to the vegetables, stirring constantly, until soup thickens. When soup is thickened, add cheese. Cook and stir until melted. Serves 4.

Hand-paint or stencil stars, hearts, or a flag design on a plain peg rack; then hang on an old-fashioned straw hat!

Simmering Soups

Turkey-Vegetable Chowder

Robyn Fiedler
Tacoma, WA

This is a terrific hearty chowder!

1/4 c. butter
2 onions, chopped
2 T. all-purpose flour
1 t. curry powder
3 c. chicken broth
1 russet potato, peeled
  and chopped
1 c. carrots, peeled and
  thinly sliced

1 c. celery, thinly sliced
2 T. fresh parsley, chopped
1/2 t. dried sage or poultry
  seasoning
3 c. cooked turkey, cubed
1-1/2 c. half-and-half
10-oz. pkg. frozen spinach

Melt butter in a large pot. Add onions and sauté for 10 minutes. Stir in flour and curry powder. Cook for 2 minutes. Add broth, potatoes, carrots, celery, parsley and sage. Reduce heat to low. Cover and simmer 15 to 20 minutes, or until vegetables are tender. Add turkey, half-and-half and frozen spinach. Cover and simmer, stirring occasionally, until heated through, about 10 to 15 minutes. Makes 4 to 6 servings.

If people concentrated on the really important things in life, there'd be a shortage of fishing poles.
– Doug Larson

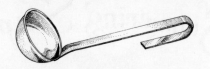

Slow-Cooker Chicken Stew

Mary Ann Nemecek
Springfield, IL

A very comforting soup any time of year...wonderful with freshly-baked bread.

2 chicken breasts, cubed
Greek seasoning to taste
2 onions, chopped
1 lb. baby carrots
6 potatoes, cubed

4-oz. can sliced mushrooms, undrained
2 10-3/4 oz. cans cream of mushroom soup

Sprinkle chicken cubes with Greek seasoning; add to a 6-quart slow cooker. Add remaining ingredients. Cover and cook on high setting for 2 hours. Turn to low setting; cook another 5 to 6 hours. Serves 6.

Friendship is a word
the very sight of
which in print makes
the heart warm.

–Augustine Birrell

Simmering Soups

Senate Bean Soup

Linda Littlejohn
Greensboro, NC

A homemade soup that's wonderful for chilly days or nights!

1 lb. dried white beans, rinsed
    and soaked
2-1/2 c. plus 3 qts. cold water,
    divided
1 ham bone

1 c. mashed potatoes
2 onions, chopped
2 c. celery, chopped
2 cloves garlic, minced
1/4 c. fresh parsley, chopped

Soak beans overnight in 2-1/2 cups cold water. Drain and put in kettle with ham bone and 3 quarts of water. Bring to a boil; reduce heat and simmer for 2 hours. Stir in potatoes, onions, celery, garlic and parsley. Simmer for approximately one hour or until beans are cooked. Remove meat from ham bone and return to soup. Serves 6 to 8.

Wisdom is the reward you
get for a lifetime of listening when
you'd have preferred to talk.

– Doug Larson

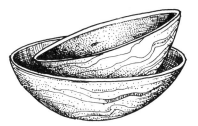

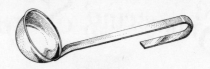

Traditional Wedding Soup

Marisa Adams
Manchester, CT

Every summer our family would travel to Pennsylvania with my cousins. The kids, nine in all, would create fun games to pass the time! Now, years later, we still try to get together, even if only for a few days.

2 qts. chicken broth	1 T. dried parsley
4 ripe tomatoes, chopped	pepper to taste
1 head escarole, chopped	Garnish: fresh parsley,
1 T. dried basil	grated Parmesan cheese

Heat broth in a large pot to a boil. Add remaining ingredients, except meatballs. Bring to a boil and add meatballs a few at a time. Bring to a boil again; reduce heat and simmer until meatballs are cooked through, about one hour. Serve with fresh parsley and Parmesan cheese sprinkled on top. Serves 8.

Meatballs:

1 lb. ground beef	1 T. dried parsley
1 egg, beaten	1/4 c. dried bread crumbs
1 clove garlic, minced	1/4 c. grated Parmesan cheese

Combine all ingredients; mix thoroughly. Roll into golf ball-size portions. Set aside until ready to add to soup mixture.

Simmering Soups

Homestyle Broccoli Soup

Pat Habiger
Spearville, KS

This really warms you up on a chilly autumn day!

1 bunch broccoli, chopped
2 c. water
1/2 c. margarine
3/4 c. onion, chopped
2 stalks celery, chopped
2 carrots, peeled and chopped
1/2 to 3/4 c. all-purpose flour

2 potatoes, peeled and chopped
2 c. milk
3 c. hot chicken broth
1 t. celery salt
1 t. garlic powder
1 T. fresh parsley, chopped
salt and pepper to taste

Steam broccoli over water until tender; reserve water. In a large soup pot, melt margarine; add onion, celery and carrots. Sauté for 3 to 5 minutes. Add flour, stirring quickly. Cook about 2 minutes over medium heat. Slowly add reserved liquid from broccoli, stirring constantly. Add broccoli and remaining ingredients. Mix well. Cook over very low heat for 1-1/2 to 2 hours stirring often to prevent scorching. Serves 4.

We all have our "good old days" tucked away inside our hearts, and we return to them in dreams like cats to favorite armchairs.

– Brian Carter

Fireside Chili

Dorothy Jackson
Weddington, NC

Every Thanksgiving for many years, our family has gathered together either at the ocean, mountains or at home to spend time together. Fireside Chili is usually cooking while the adults are catching up on events within the family and the children are running around! No matter when or where this chili is served, it will always remind me of these special family times together.

1-1/2 lbs. ground beef or pork
1 c. green pepper, chopped
1 c. onion, chopped
2 15-oz. cans red kidney
    beans, drained
28-oz. can tomatoes, chopped
15-oz. can tomato sauce
1-1/2 c. water
2 T. chili powder

2 T. Worcestershire sauce
1 T. honey
1 t. salt
1/2 t. dried basil
1/2 t. cinnamon
1/4 t. ground allspice
1 bay leaf

In a 4-quart Dutch oven, cook meat with green pepper and onion until meat is browned and vegetables are tender. Drain; add kidney beans, undrained tomatoes and remaining ingredients. Simmer, uncovered, for 30 minutes. Cover and simmer for one hour, stirring occasionally. Discard bay leaf. Serves 6 to 8.

Heaven is a pot of chili
simmering on the stove.

–Charles Simic

Hearty Minestrone

Teresa Sullivan
Westerville, OH

This soup is worth the extra time it takes to prepare...
you may even want to double the recipe!

1/2 c. dried kidney beans, rinsed
    and soaked
2 slices bacon, diced
1/4 lb. cooked ham, diced
1/2 lb. Italian sausage
    link, diced
1 onion, chopped
3 cloves garlic, chopped
3 stalks celery, chopped
1 leek, chopped
2 zucchini, chopped

2 qts. beef broth
1/2 head cabbage, shredded
1 c. dry red wine
16-oz. can whole tomatoes,
    cut up
1/2 c. elbow macaroni,
    uncooked
pepper to taste
2 t. dried basil
Garnish: grated Parmesan
    cheese, grated

Soak beans with water; let stand overnight. Cook bacon, ham and sausage in a large skillet. Add onion, garlic, celery, leek and zucchini. Cook for 10 minutes. Heat broth in a large kettle. Add bacon mixture, drained kidney beans, cabbage and wine. Simmer, partially covered, for 90 minutes. Add tomatoes, macaroni, pepper and basil. Cook for 15 minutes. Serve with cheese. Makes 6 to 8 servings.

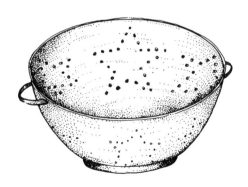

Where we love is home...home that our feet may leave,
but not our hearts.
– Oliver Wendell Holmes, Sr.

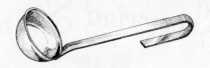

Mama's Vegetable Beef Soup

Alicia Bates
Kent, OH

I can remember coming home after school and smelling the aroma of this soup and homemade bread. Even today it still takes me back!

1 lb. ground beef
3 c. water
1 c. carrots, peeled and sliced
1 c. celery, chopped
1 c. onion, chopped
2 c. potatoes, peeled and diced
1 t. salt

1 t. browning and seasoning
  sauce
1/4 t. pepper
1 t. dried basil
1 bay leaf
28-oz. can whole tomatoes

Sauté ground beef, breaking up with a spoon until well browned. Drain well. Stir in remaining ingredients. Heat to boiling, reduce heat. Cover and simmer 20 minutes or until veggies are tender. Remove bay leaf before serving. Makes 6 servings.

One of the oldest human needs is having someone to wonder where you are when you don't come home at night.

– Margaret Mead

Simmering Soups

Camp Stew

Peg Ackerman
Pasadena, CA

On a cool, fall evening, I always make this recipe. It's wonderful
for a family campout or informal dinner with friends.

1 c. biscuit baking mix
salt and pepper to taste
4 lbs. stew beef cubes
2 to 3 T. butter
1-1/2 to 2 lbs. carrots, trimmed

6 to 7 russet potatoes, halved
  or quartered
2 onions, quartered
2 envs. stew seasoning mix

Add biscuit mix to a large plastic zipping bag; season with salt and pepper. Add beef cubes, a few at a time; shake to coat well. Working in batches, melt butter in a large skillet; add beef to skillet and brown on all sides. Transfer browned beef to a large roasting pan. Add carrots, potatoes and onions; add enough water to cover. Sprinkle with seasoning mix. Cover and bake in oven at 350 degrees for 1-1/2 to 2 hours, or on camp stove for 2 to 2-1/2 hours, until meat and potatoes are tender. Add more water as needed. Serves 10 to 12.

Stencil the alphabet on the outside of an old wooden wagon,
then tuck in your children's teddy bears or dolls!

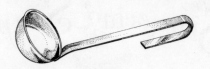

Minnesota Wild Rice Soup

Maureen Noterman
Adams, MN

*We love this thick, rice soup. It really takes the chill out
on the cool evenings we get here in Minnesota!*

1/2 c. wild rice, uncooked	4 c. chicken broth
2 c. cold water	3 T. cornstarch
1/4 c. butter	2-1/4 c. milk, divided
2/3 c. onions, chopped	salt and pepper to taste
2/3 c. celery, chopped	
2/3 c. carrots, peeled and chopped	

Soak rice in cold water for one to 2 hours; drain. Meanwhile, melt
butter in a large saucepan. Add vegetables and sauté for 3 minutes.
Add rice and sauté for 5 minutes, stirring occasionally. Add chicken
broth. Cover and bring to a boil. Reduce heat. Simmer for one hour, or
until rice and vegetables are tender. Slowly add 2 cups milk to hot
soup; mix well. Dissolve cornstarch in 1/4 cup of remaining cold milk.
Whisk into soup; bring to a boil. Simmer until thickened. Add salt and
pepper to taste. Serves 4 to 6.

*Layer potpourri ingredients in one of
Grandma's old, wavy glass jars! Tie a
square of homespun on the top with
raffia and add a rusty tin star or
heart...beautiful!*

Simmering Soups

Aunt Sandy's Special Chowder
Wendy Lee Paffenroth
Pine Island, NY

This makes the house smell so good! We love to serve it with homemade muffins or crusty Italian bread.

5 slices bacon, diced
5 c. water
1 c. celery, diced
28-oz. can stewed tomatoes
3 potatoes, peeled and sliced
4 carrots, diced
3 onions, diced

2 T. fresh parsley, chopped
1 t. dried thyme
1 t. salt
1/2 t. pepper
1 bay leaf
2 10-oz. cans minced or
   whole clams, undrained

In a heavy Dutch oven, fry bacon until almost crisp. Add remaining ingredients except clams. Heat until boiling and reduce the heat to a low simmer. Cover and cook until the vegetables are tender. Add clams and juice; cook about another 20 to 30 minutes. Serves 6.

Of soup and love, the first is best.

– Spanish Proverb

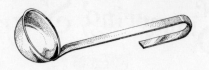

Corn & Sausage Chowder

Kim McGeorge
Ashley, OH

Fresh corn makes this soup so wonderful!

2 c. fresh corn kernels
1 lb. ground pork sausage
1 c. onions, chopped
4 c. potatoes, peeled and diced
2 c. water
1/2 t. dried marjoram

2 t. salt
1/8 t. pepper
16-oz. can cream-style corn
12-oz. can evaporated milk
Garnish: chopped fresh parsley

Cook corn in boiling water 4 to 5 minutes; drain and set aside to cool. In a skillet, brown sausage over medium heat for 5 minutes; drain. Add onions; continue cooking 3 more minutes. Add potatoes, water and seasonings. Bring to a boil, reduce heat to simmer and cook until potatoes are tender. Add both fresh and cream-style corn and evaporated milk. Heat to almost boiling. Ladle chowder into bowls; garnish with parsley. Serves 6.

Create the feel of an old general store by filling a wooden bowl with dried apple and orange slices, cinnamon sticks, rosehips, cloves and star anise; tuck in a wooden or antique scoop.

PATCHWORK
Salads

A summer delight...baskets filled with sun-ripened tomatoes, crisp lettuce, crunchy carrots and red radishes! I can picture Mom's kitchen table, covered with a blue and white checked cloth. Pink and white cosmos in a green enamel pitcher, tall glasses filled to the brim with ice, and a pitcher of tea complete the memory.

Certain country things seem just right in summertime...a salad of just-picked vegetables and an icy glass of tea. These wonderful vegetables never taste the same in winter as they do in summer, fresh from the garden.

Our family always sat on the porch after lunch. Locusts filled the afternoon with their song, a sure sign that summer was moving toward fall. Before evening came, the kids would wade barefoot through the creek, splash one another and enjoy the cool water in the late summer heat.

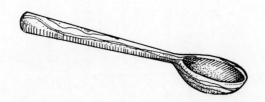

Patchwork Salads

Summertime Spaghetti Salad

Mary Haubiel
Delaware, OH

We always enjoy this salad at family gatherings or barbecues...
it's become a family tradition!

1 lb. linguine pasta, uncooked
16-oz. bottle Italian salad
   dressing
1 green pepper, chopped
2 bunches green onions, diced

4-oz. jar sliced mushrooms,
   drained
1/4 to 1/2 lb. cooked ham, diced
Optional: 1-oz. jar salad
   seasoning

Cook pasta according to package directions; drain. Combine remaining ingredients well and toss with cooled pasta. Refrigerate overnight, or at least 12 hours. Serves 8.

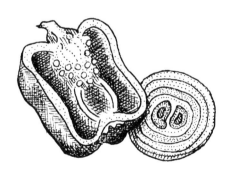

Slip small, old-fashioned iron hooks over a twig or narrow length of barn siding...a wonderful primitive herb rack!

Cherry Tomato Salad

Kathy Williamson
Delaware, OH

I like this salad because I always have the ingredients on hand and it's so simple to make.

1 lb. cherry tomatoes
2 T. fresh chives, chopped
1 T. fresh mint, finely chopped

1 t. sugar
salt and pepper to taste
2 T. white wine vinegar

Slice tomatoes onto a pretty serving dish. Sprinkle with remaining ingredients. Serves 4.

Homemade Blue Cheese Dressing

Pat Akers
Stanton, CA

Salads will never be the same after you taste this fresh dressing!

4 c. mayonnaise
2 c. buttermilk
1 T. onion powder
1 T. seasoned salt

1 T. coarse pepper
4-oz. container crumbled
  blue cheese

Place mayonnaise in a large mixing bowl; slowly blend in buttermilk. Add remaining ingredients one at a time. Keeps in the refrigerator for 10 days. Makes 6 cups.

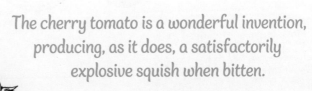

The cherry tomato is a wonderful invention, producing, as it does, a satisfactorily explosive squish when bitten.

– Miss Manners

Patchwork Salads

Carrot & Raisin Salad

Jackie Crough
Salina, KS

Grandma made this salad often. It's always very good!

2 c. carrots, peeled and shredded
1 c. raisins
1/2 c. chopped walnuts

1/2 c. mayonnaise
Garnish: lettuce leaves

Mix all ingredients except garnish together in a large bowl. Cover and refrigerate overnight. Serve on a bed of lettuce. Serves 4.

Vermicelli Salad

Judy Kelly
St. Charles, MO

Quick and so easy!

1 lb. vermicelli pasta, uncooked
4 T. oil
1 t. lemon juice
4-oz. jar chopped pimentos,
  drained

1/2 c. onion, chopped
1 green pepper, chopped
16-oz. jar mayonnaise
salt, pepper and garlic salt
  to taste

Cook pasta according to package directions. Rinse and drain. Add oil and lemon juice; refrigerate overnight. The next day, add remaining ingredients, chill and serve. Makes 8 servings.

Paint an old wicker basket mustard yellow, line it with a square of blue homespun and share the extra bounty from your garden with a friend.

Fruit Trifle Salad

Mary Tolle
Upland, CA

This is always my favorite to serve in summer when strawberries are fresh and plentiful.

6 oranges, peeled and sliced
3 bananas, sliced
3 c. blueberries
2 c. seedless grapes
3 c. strawberries, hulled
and halved

3.4-oz. pkg. instant vanilla
pudding mix
1-3/4 c. milk
3/4 c. sour cream
1 t. orange zest

In a large glass bowl, layer all of the fruit in order listed above. Fruit can be substituted for in-season items, except melon. For the topping, combine pudding mix and milk. Beat for one to 2 minutes. Beat in sour cream and orange zest. Serve with fruit. Makes 10 to 15 servings.

Where is home? Home is where
the heart can laugh
without shyness.
Home is where the
heart's tears can dry at
their own pace.

–Vernon G. Baker

Patchwork Salads

Vegetable Pasta Salad

Susan Kennedy
Delaware, OH

*So easy to make and even better when you use fresh,
crunchy vegetables from your garden!*

1/4 c. fresh parsley sprigs,
   loosely packed
2 T. salad oil
2 T. wine vinegar
2 T. water
1 to 2 cloves garlic, chopped
1/2 t. dry mustard
1/4 t. salt
1/4 t. pepper
2 oz. linguine noodles,
   uncooked and broken

1 carrot, peeled and cut into
   julienne strips
1 turnip, peeled and cut into
   julienne strips
1 zucchini, cut into
   julienne strips
1/2 c. frozen or fresh peas
1/2 c. shredded mozzarella
   cheese

To prepare dressing, combine parsley, salad oil, wine vinegar, water, garlic, mustard, salt and pepper in a blender. Blend until combined. Set aside. Cook linguine according to package directions. Drain; rinse with cold water and drain again. In a large salad bowl, combine pasta, carrot, turnip, zucchini, peas and cheese. Add dressing; toss to coat. Serves 6 to 8.

Homemade preserves are
beautiful displayed in an
old-fashioned corner cupboard!
Bright red tomatoes, green
pickles and golden corn are
particularly nice.

Sunflower Strawberry Salad

Shirley Moteberg
Grandin, ND

This recipe makes a large bowl...just perfect for a family reunion!

2 c. strawberries, hulled and
    sliced
1 apple, cored and diced
1 c. seedless green grapes,
    halved

1/2 c. celery, thinly sliced
1/4 c. raisins
1/2 c. strawberry yogurt
2 T. sunflower kernels
Optional: lettuce leaves

In a large bowl, combine fruit, celery and raisins. Stir in yogurt. Cover
and chill one hour. Sprinkle with sunflower kernels just before serving.
Spoon over lettuce leaves, if desired. Makes 6 servings.

I value the friend who for me finds time on his calendar, but I
cherish the friend who for me does not consult his calendar.

– Robert Brault

Patchwork Salads

Banana Salad

Phyllis Laughrey
Mount Vernon, OH

Refreshing and cool, a great warm-weather fruit salad.

2 3-oz. pkgs. lemon gelatin mix
2 c. boiling water
2 c. cold water or lemon-lime
    soda
1 c. mini marshmallows

2 bananas, diced
20-oz. can crushed pineapple,
    drained
1 c. frozen whipped topping,
    thawed

Dissolve gelatin in boiling water. Add cold water or lemon-lime soda.
Add marshmallows and allow them to melt. Let set until thick and
completely cooled. Add bananas and pineapple to gelatin mixture.
Let it set completely. Fold whipped topping into cooked custard and
spread on top of set gelatin. Serves 15.

Custard:

1 c. pineapple juice
1/2 c. sugar
1 T. flour

1/8 t. salt
1 egg

Cook pineapple juice, sugar, flour, salt and egg until thick. Set aside
to cool.

*Few things are more delightful than grandchildren
fighting over your lap.*

– Doug Larson

Susie Salad

Sue Lovely
Three Rivers, MI

A recipe handed down to me from my mom;
now it's "expected" at most meals!

1 head lettuce, torn
1/2 c. onion, chopped
8-oz. pkg. shredded Swiss
   cheese

10-oz. box frozen peas
salt and pepper to taste
Optional: grated Parmesan
   cheese to taste

Layer above ingredients except cheese in a salad bowl. Cover with dressing. Don't mix until ready to serve. Best if refrigerated overnight before serving. Sprinkle Parmesan cheese over dressing if desired. Serves 8.

Dressing:

1/2 c. mayonnaise-style
   salad dressing

2 T. sour cream
2 T. sugar

Combine all ingredients.

Fill an old sap bucket
with blooms from
your garden, attach
a loop of ribbon and hang
it from your doorknob...
a lovely way to
welcome visitors!

Patchwork Salads

Twelve-Layer Salad

Kristi Warzocha
Lakewood, OH

Layer this salad in a glass bowl so the variety of colors can be seen!

3/4 lb. fresh peas
1 head iceberg lettuce, shredded
3/4 c. fresh parsley, chopped
4 eggs, hard-boiled, peeled
    and chopped
1 red pepper, thinly sliced
4 carrots, peeled and shredded
1 c. black olives, sliced

2 T. fresh dill, chopped
1 c. radishes, sliced
3 c. shredded Swiss or Cheddar
    cheese, shredded
1/2 lb. bacon, crisply cooked
    and crumbled
1 red onion, thinly sliced

Cook peas in water until crisp-tender; set aside. Line the bottom of a 3-quart, straight-sided bowl with lettuce. Layer the remaining ingredients in the order listed, adding peas after black olives. Spread half of the dressing over the salad, set aside the remaining dressing to serve on the side. Sprinkle salad with remaining parsley. Cover bowl tightly with plastic wrap and refrigerate for 6 to 12 hours. Serves 10 to 12.

Dressing:

2 c. mayonnaise
1/2 c. sour cream
1/4 c. fresh chives, chopped
2 T. sugar

1 T. tarragon vinegar
salt and pepper to taste
1/2 c. plus 2 T. fresh parsley,
    chopped and divided

Combine all dressing ingredients and 1/2 cup parsley.

A child on a farm sees a plane fly overhead and dreams of a faraway place. A traveler on the plane sees the farm house... and dreams of home.

– Carl Burns

Mom's Potato Salad

Jane Goetz
Hays, KS

This recipe reminds me of family get-togethers and camping trips.
Every time I make it, I remember Mom and how special
she was and is to me.

5 lbs. redskin potatoes, cooked
   and diced
1 doz. eggs, hard-boiled, peeled
   and diced
3 T. sugar
3 T. mustard

3 T. horseradish sauce
5 T. dill pickle juice
yellow food coloring, if desired
32-oz. jar mayonnaise
1/2 c. onion, chopped

Combine potatoes and eggs in a large bowl. In a separate container, mix all the sauce ingredients together. Pour over the potatoes and eggs and mix well. Refrigerate a few hours before serving. Makes 12 servings.

Let first the onion flourish there,
Rose among the roots, the maiden fair.
Wine-scented and poetic soul
Of the capacious salad bowl!

–Robert Louis Stevenson

Patchwork Salads

Red Potato Salad

Katie Sullivan
Westerville, OH

A traditional redskin potato salad we like to serve with grilled dishes.

12 redskin potatoes, diced
2 T. French or Russian salad
    dressing
1-1/2 c. celery, chopped
8 to 10 green onions, chopped
1/2 red onion, chopped
1/4 green pepper, finely chopped
1/4 red pepper, finely chopped
1/4 c. sweet pickles, finely
    chopped

1/4 c. fresh parsley, finely
    chopped
3 T. fresh chives, finely chopped
7 eggs, hard-boiled and peeled
2 t. salt
fresh ground pepper to taste
2/3 c. mayonnaise
Garnish: paprika and parsley

Boil potatoes in water until just tender. Drain and rinse briefly in cold water to stop cooking process. Toss in French or Russian dressing and chill at least 30 minutes. Combine celery, onions, peppers, pickles, parsley and chives with the marinated potatoes. Chop 5 of the eggs, reserving the other 2 for garnish. Add to salad, along with salt, pepper and mayonnaise. Check seasoning. Refrigerate at least 3 hours or overnight. Check seasoning again. Transfer to a serving bowl. Slice remaining 2 eggs and decorate top, sprinkling with paprika and chopped parsley. Serves 8.

Traveling in the company of those we love is home in motion.

– Leigh Hunt

Cranberry Salad

Diane Dodd
Cape Girardeau, MO

I remember this salad so well because my brother and I were very young when it became a tradition to have cranberry salad every Thanksgiving and Christmas. Now, for many years, I've been bringing it to our family gatherings.

16-oz. pkg. frozen cranberries
1-1/2 c. sugar
1/2 pt. whipping cream
1 c. mini marshmallows

1-1/2 c. apples, cored and diced
1 c. white grapes, halved
1 c. chopped nuts

Rinse frozen cranberries under cold running water to wash off any loose stems. Grind or chop frozen cranberries using a food processor or blender. Put chopped cranberries in a large bowl and add sugar. Thoroughly mix by hand and refrigerate overnight. Before serving, beat whipping cream in a separate bowl until peaks form. Fold whipped cream into the cranberry-sugar mixture. Add the marshmallows, apples, grapes and nuts. Mix together and serve. Makes 8 to 10 servings.

Family faces are magic mirrors. Looking at people who belong to us, we see the past, present and future. We make discoveries about ourselves.

– Gail Lumet Buckley

Patchwork Salads

Sugar Snap Pea & Bean Salad

Liz Kenneweg
Delaware, OH

Freshly-picked beans and peas from your garden make this salad perfect for a warm weather cookout with family and friends!

Dressing:

1 clove garlic, minced
1/4 t. salt
2 T. red wine vinegar
2 t. Dijon mustard

1/8 t. sugar
1/4 c. olive oil
pepper to taste

Place garlic in a small bowl along with salt, vinegar, mustard and sugar. Mix well; slowly add the olive oil, whisking constantly. Season with pepper and set aside.

Salad:

1/2 lb. green beans
1/2 lb. wax beans
1/4 lb. sugar snap peas
1 shallot, sliced lengthwise and
   cut into thin strips

3 ripe tomatoes, cut into
   one-inch cubes
3/4 c. fresh basil leaves
salt and pepper to taste

Add green beans to a stockpot; cover with water. Bring to a boil and cook until just tender, 3 to 5 minutes. Remove beans with a slotted spoon and drain well; rinse under cold water and drain again. Repeat cooking instructions for both the wax beans and peas. When beans and peas are cooked, pat dry and place in a large bowl. Add shallot and tomatoes. Chop basil by layering the leaves then rolling them together. Slice very thinly and add to the salad. Sprinkle with salt and pepper and toss well. When ready to serve, toss with dressing. Serves 4 to 6.

Orange-Cranberry Salad

Beth Warner
Delaware, OH

*My grandma always made this during the holidays. It has such
a refreshing sweet-tart taste!*

6 c. fresh cranberries
1 orange, sliced
2 c. sugar
1 c. celery, coarsely chopped

1 c. English walnuts, chopped
2 3-oz. pkgs. lemon gelatin mix
3-1/2 c. boiling water

Grind cranberries and orange together. Stir in sugar and allow mixture
to stand overnight. The next morning, add celery and nuts. Set aside.
Dissolve gelatin in boiling water. Set it aside to cool. Stir into cranberry
mixture. Chill until firm. Serves 8 to 10.

A great flea-market find! A weathered door shutter gives
a primitive feel when hung over a window, or attach
two shutters together for a wonderful room divider.

Cookie Salad

Crystal Moeller
Hebo, OR

Whenever I make this recipe it reminds me of a dear friend,
who first shared it with our family.

2 3-oz. pkgs. vanilla instant
  pudding mix
1 c. buttermilk
8-oz. container frozen whipped
  topping, thawed

15-oz. can fruit cocktail
2 15-oz. cans mandarin oranges
20-oz. can pineapple tidbits
1 pkg. fudge stripe cookies,
  crushed and divided

Mix pudding mix and buttermilk. Fold in whipped topping. Drain all of the fruit. Separate maraschino cherries from the fruit cocktail and set aside. Add fruit to pudding mixture and mix well. Blend in cookies, reserving 1/2 cup. Sprinkle top of salad with reserved crushed cookies and top with reserved maraschino cherries. Serves 8 to 10.

An old wooden bowl full of colorful, fresh fruit makes
a terrific warm-weather centerpiece.

Shimmering Three-Berry Salad

Jo Ann
Gooseberry Patch

Berry picking is a fun family outing! Gather everyone together and spend the afternoon picking your favorite berries for this fresh berry-filled salad!

2 c. cranberry juice
2 3-oz. pkgs. gelatin mix,
   any red flavor

1-1/2 c. club soda
1 t. lemon juice
3 c. assorted berries, divided

Bring cranberry juice to a boil; stir in gelatin until completely dissolved. Stir in club soda and lemon juice. Refrigerate about 1-1/2 hours, until thickened. Stir in 2 cups of the berries. Spoon into a 5-cup mold. Refrigerate 4 hours or until firm. Unmold. Top with remaining berries. Serves 8.

Silences make the real conversations between friends. Not the saying but the never needing to say is what counts.

– Margaret Lee Runbeck

Patchwork Salads

Ribbon Salad

Doris Stegner
Delaware, OH

This pretty salad is well worth the time it takes to prepare it...
it's very attractive sliced!

6 c. water   16-oz. carton sour cream
6 3-oz. boxes gelatin mix,
  different flavors and colors

Bring water to a boil. Dissolve one box of gelatin in one cup boiling water. Reserve 1/3 cup gelatin mixture and pour remaining gelatin into an 8" square dish. When gelatin is set, mix the reserved 1/3 cup of gelatin with 1/3 cup of sour cream and spread over set gelatin. When the sour cream layer has set, repeat layering with the remaining ingredients until salad has 12 layers. Serves 8.

On days when warmth is the most important need of
the human heart, the kitchen is the place you
can find it.

– E. B. White

Marinated Vegetables

The Governor's Inn
Ludlow, VT

It's easy to make your own dressing, and it tastes so fresh!
Serve as an appetizer, or as a meatless meal.

1/2 lb. cheese tortellini, cooked
   and drained
1 c. broccoli flowerets
1 c. cauliflower flowerets
20-oz. can pineapple chunks,
   drained

6-oz. can pitted black olives,
   drained
1 red pepper, cut into strips

Combine all ingredients in a large bowl. Cover with poppy seed dressing and toss gently to coat. Marinate for several hours. Serve as an appetizer, or as a whole meal. Serves 6 to 8.

Poppy Seed House Dressing:

1 c. sugar
2/3 c. white vinegar
1 T. salt

1 T. dry mustard
1 c. oil
2 T. poppy seeds

Combine first 4 ingredients in a blender and blend. Drop by drop, add the oil until it is incorporated. Add the poppy seed.

Lettuce is divine, although I'm not sure
it is really a food.

– Diana Vreeland

Overnight Salad

Phyllis Laughrey
Mount Vernon, OH

Save time by preparing this easy salad the night before!

10-oz. container frozen peas
1-1/2 c. mayonnaise
1/2 c. radishes, sliced
1/2 c. onion, chopped
1 head lettuce, torn
1 c. celery, chopped

1/2 c. green pepper, chopped
1 T. sugar
1 lb. bacon, crisply cooked
  and crumbled
1/2 c. shredded Cheddar cheese

Cook peas in boiling water for one minute. Drain and set aside to cool. In a large bowl, combine mayonnaise with radishes and onions; mix with peas. Layer remaining ingredients in order listed. Top with bacon and cheese, cover and refrigerate overnight before serving. Makes 8 to 10 servings.

I loved my vegetable garden,
so here is my sad ballad:
I nurtured it for months and
ate it in one salad.

–Arnold Zarett

Caesar Salad

Vickie
Gooseberry Patch

*Our family likes this version, created from the traditional
Caesar salad recipe.*

3 cloves garlic, peeled and
   halved
4 thick slices Italian bread
5 T. olive oil, civided
3 T. mayonnaise
3 T. lemon juice

1/4 t. salt
1/4 t. pepper
1 head romaine lettuce, torn
   into pieces
1/4 c. grated Parmesan cheese

Use 2 cloves of the garlic and rub the slices of bread on both sides.
Brush bread with 2 tablespoons oil and cut into 1/2-inch cubes. Spread
cubes on an ungreased baking sheet and bake at 400 degrees for
10 minutes, tossing occasionally, until golden and crisp. Rub remaining
garlic clove on the inside of a large chilled bowl. Combine mayonnaise,
lemon juice, salt, pepper and remaining oil; whisk until smooth. Add
romaine, Parmesan cheese, and croutons; toss until well coated.
Serves 4.

Life is too short to bother with
tasteless tomatoes.

– Cindy Pawlcyn

Patchwork Salads

Chicken Salad

Rosemary Montgomery
High Bridge, NJ

My favorite recipe because it's so pretty and delicious, too!

6 boneless, skinless chicken
   breasts
1 T. fresh parsley, chopped
1 t. fresh dill, chopped
2 T. green pepper, chopped
2 T. celery, chopped
1/3 c. carrots, peeled and
   chopped

2/3 c. chopped walnuts
1 t. crushed pepper
mayonnaise to desired
   consistency
salt to taste
Garnish: lettuce leaves

Simmer chicken in water until done, about 1-1/2 hours. Cut chicken into bite-size cubes. Combine chicken, parsley, dill, green pepper, celery, carrots, walnuts and pepper. Add mayonnaise to desired consistency and salt to taste. Refrigerate a few hours and serve in a decorative bowl lined with leaves of lettuce. Serves 4.

I want to go home to the dull old town, with the shaded street and the open square; and the hill and the flats and the house I love and the paths I know, I want to go home.

– Paul Kester

Family Reunion Fruit Salad

*Debbie Cummons-Parker
Lakeview, OH*

One of our family favorites. It was found in an old-fashioned church cookbook!

15-oz. can fruit cocktail
15-oz. can mandarin oranges
20-oz. can crushed pineapple

3-oz. pkg. instant vanilla
   pudding mix

Drain fruits, reserving the syrup. Add pudding mix to the drained fruits and stir well. Add enough of reserved fruit syrup to moisten to desired consistency. Serves 6.

Summertime Salad

*Margaret Scoresby
Mount Vernon, OH*

There's nothing like fresh tomatoes from the garden for this recipe!

2/3 c. canola or olive oil
1/2 t. salt
1 minced garlic clove
pepper to taste
1/4 c. salad vinegar

3 T. fresh basil, chopped
1/4 c. onion, chopped
1-1/2 c. mozzarella cheese cubes
1 pt. cherry tomatoes, halved

Whisk together first 5 ingredients well; toss in remaining ingredients. Chill until ready to serve. Serves 4.

Stencil a collection of Shaker boxes in country colors of barn red, mustard, moss green, and navy. Tuck some homemade cookies and your favorite recipe inside... perfect for a new neighbor!

Family-style
Casseroles

Hearing Mom's voice call us for dinner was always a welcome sound! We hopped out of the swing, dropped our bikes, or ran in from the barn as quickly as we could! It was always understood that Mom would prepare the dinner, and the kids would stay out of the kitchen until called on to fill water glasses, set the table, or bring an extra chair.

The aroma coming from the kitchen was always something special...a combination of sage, spices, chicken and biscuits; each of Mom's casseroles were a masterpiece!

The best part about gathering together for dinner was the company of extended family. Cousins, nephews, nieces, even dogs came to share in the fun, and there was always room at the table for new friends. That has always been the best part of family dinners... when family & friends get together to share.

Family·style Casseroles

Shepherd's Pie

Barbara Arnold
Toledo, OH

A truly old-fashioned dish. Try mashing your potatoes with sour cream and cream cheese...wonderful!

1 lb. ground beef
1/4 c. onion, chopped
1/2 t. salt
1 env. brown gravy mix
10-oz. pkg. frozen peas and
   carrots

1/2 t. dried basil leaves
1/4 c. shredded Cheddar cheese
1-1/2 c. mashed potatoes,
   seasoned and warmed

Cook ground beef and onion over medium-high heat until beef is browned and onion is tender. Sprinkle with salt. Prepare gravy mix according to package directions and add to beef mixture. After gravy thickens, add frozen vegetables and basil. Cover and simmer for 5 minutes. Pour into a 1-1/2 quart casserole dish. Fold cheese into mashed potatoes. Spread evenly over top of casserole. Bake at 450 degrees for 15 minutes or until potatoes are lightly browned on top. Serves 4.

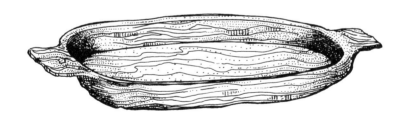

The golden rule of friendship is to listen to others
as you would have them listen to you.

–David Augsburger

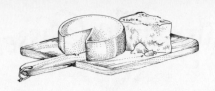

Shrimp with Garlic

Cheryl Bierley
Miamisburg, OH

This recipe is dear to me because it reminds me of the special occasions in my childhood. Mom would prepare this dish for family birthdays, graduations and when our family was expecting company. It's a bit fancy, but quite simple to make.

1 c. butter, melted
2 cloves garlic, minced
1/3 c. fresh parsley, chopped
1/2 t. paprika
1/8 t. cayenne pepper
1/2 c. cooking sherry or
   white wine

2 c. soft bread crumbs
5 to 6 c. shrimp, cleaned and
   cooked
Garnish: chopped fresh parsley

To melted butter add garlic, parsley, paprika, cayenne pepper and sherry or wine. Mix thoroughly. Add bread crumbs and toss. Arrange shrimp in an 11"x7" baking pan. Spoon the butter mixture over the shrimp. Bake at 325 degrees for 25 minutes or until crumbs brown. Sprinkle additional chopped parsley over top before serving.
Makes 4 to 6 servings.

Basically the only thing we need is a hand
that rests on our own, that wishes it well,
that sometimes guides us.

–Hector Bianciotti

Red Beans & Rice Casserole

Sandy Spayer
Jeromesville, OH

A hearty dish that will satisfy the whole family.

2 c. dried red kidney beans,
   rinsed and sorted
1 T. oil
8-oz. pkg. hot Italian ground
   pork sausage
1 yellow onion, chopped
1 green pepper, chopped
1/2 c. celery, chopped
2 cloves garlic, minced
1/2 lb. smoked ham, diced

4 c. beef broth
2 bay leaves
1/2 t. dried thyme
1/2 t. dried marjoram
1/4 t. cayenne pepper
2 c. long-grain rice, cooked
1 T. red wine vinegar
1/2 t. salt
Optional: hot pepper sauce

Place beans in a 6-quart Dutch oven and cover with water; soak beans overnight. Drain beans and set aside. Heat oil in Dutch oven; add Italian sausage and sauté until brown. Remove and place on paper towels to drain. Remove all but 2 tablespoons of pan drippings. Combine onion, green pepper, celery and garlic; sauté until tender. Add reserved beans, ham, broth, bay leaves, thyme, marjoram and cayenne. Over high heat, bring ingredients to a boil. Reduce heat to low and simmer, covered, until beans are tender, about 1-1/2 hours. Discard bay leaves. Drain bean mixture, reserving one cup liquid. Place bean mixture and reserved liquid into a lightly greased 3-quart casserole dish. Stir in rice, vinegar and salt to taste. Bake, covered, at 350 degrees for 30 minutes. Serves 6.

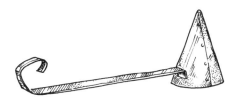

Hang an old-fashioned wooden pitchfork by the back door...
a handy hat rack!

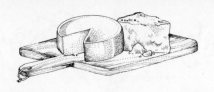

Chicken Tetrazzini

Debbie Musick
Yukon, OK

This recipe came from one of my mother's best friends: "Aunt" Cathryn. She always served it for holiday dinners and now my mother makes it for us. Each time we visit our mother, she serves it or has it in a casserole dish for us to take home and bake. I have wonderful memories of "Aunt" Cathryn; when we make this recipe, it brings her back for awhile.

1 c. onion, minced
2 T. butter
2 10-3/4 oz. cans cream of
   mushroom soup
2 10-3/4 oz. cans cream of
   chicken soup
8-oz. pkg. Old English cheese
1/2 c. milk
1/2 c. water
1 t. curry powder
1/4 t. dried thyme

1/8 t. dried basil
1/4 t. dried oregano
2 7-oz. pkgs. spaghetti noodles,
   cooked
5-lb. chicken, cooked and cubed
4-oz. jar sliced pimentos,
   drained
salt and pepper to taste
Garnish: grated Parmesan
   cheese

Sauté onion in butter. Add soups, cheese, milk, water and spices. Add spaghetti to soup mixture; fold in chicken and pimentos. Spoon into two, 13"x9" baking pans. Add salt and pepper to taste; top with grated cheese. Bake at 350 degrees for 45 minutes.
Serves 8 to 10.

Babies are always more trouble
than you thought...and
more wonderful.

–Charles Osgood

Family-style Casseroles

Steak & Potatoes

Anita McClard
Pelion, SC

*I like this recipe because it's perfect for round steak
and can easily be prepared in my slow cooker, too.*

3 T. all-purpose flour
salt and pepper to taste
3-lb. beef round steak
1/2 c. onion, chopped
1 T. shortening
7 potatoes

2 10-3/4 oz. cream of
    mushroom soup
1 c. milk
4-1/2 oz. can button
    mushrooms, drained

In a medium bowl, combine flour, salt and pepper. Cut steak into
2-inch pieces; dip steak in flour to coat. In a skillet, brown steak and
onion in a small amount of shortening. Set aside. Peel and slice
potatoes in 1/8-inch thick pieces. Cover potatoes with water; boil for
only 2 minutes. Mix mushroom soup with milk. Layer potatoes, steak
and soup mixture, ending with soup. Sprinkle with mushrooms. Bake
at 300 degrees for 2 hours. Serves 4.

The best things you can give
children, next to good habits,
are good memories.

–Sydney J. Harris

Onion & Cheese Casserole

Kristi Warzocha
Lakewood, OH

Combining sweet onions and cheese make this casserole delicious!

2 c. butter-flavored crackers,
  crushed and divided
1/2 c. butter, divided
3 lbs. onions, sliced
2 T. all-purpose flour
1/2 t. salt
1/2 t. ground pepper

2 c. milk
1/2 lb. pasteurized process
  cheese, diced
Garnish: red pepper,
  cut into rings

Layer one cup cracker crumbs in a lightly oiled 11"x8" baking pan; set aside. In a skillet, melt 1/4 cup of butter. Stir in onions, cooking until tender. Spoon onions over cracker crumbs. Melt remaining butter and stir in flour, salt, and pepper. Stir constantly and cook for one minute. Blend in milk gradually. Continue to stir well and cook until mixture is thick. Add cheese and stir until mixture is smooth. Pour over onions; sprinkle with remaining cracker crumbs. Bake at 350 degrees for 25 to 30 minutes or until lightly browned. Garnish with red pepper rings. Serves 12.

Life is like an onion, you peel it
off one layer at a time, and sometimes
you weep.

–Carl Sandburg

Baked Chicken & Wild Rice

Michele MacIntyre
Placerville, CA

Our family loves this because it tastes great and is so simple to prepare. We make it the night before and I just put it in the oven when I get home from work.

10-3/4 oz. can cream of chicken soup
10-3/4 oz. can cream of celery soup
1 pkg. onion soup mix
1-1/4 c. white or red wine

2 6-oz. pkgs. long-grain & wild rice mix
4 boneless, skinless, chicken breasts, cut into bite-size pieces

In a large bowl, combine soups, onion soup mix and wine. Mix together thoroughly. Add 2 packages of wild rice mix; do not use seasoning packets included in packages. Mix well. Place rice mixture in a 13"x9" baking pan. Place chicken on top of rice mixture. Cover dish with aluminum foil and place in refrigerator overnight. Bake at 350 degrees for one to 2 hours, until chicken is thoroughly cooked. Serves 4 to 6.

Hang a small berry wreath on your
cupboard doorknobs!

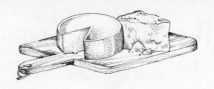

Spaghetti Pie

Eleanor Bierley
Miamisburg, OH

A great family meal; just add a salad and some garlic bread!

8-oz. pkg. spaghetti, cooked
2 eggs, beaten
1/4 c. grated Parmesan cheese
1/2 t. salt
1/4 lb. pepperoni, sliced and
    divided

2 c. shredded mozzarella cheese,
    divided
2 c. spaghetti sauce, warmed

Combine spaghetti, eggs, Parmesan cheese, and salt. Mix thoroughly. Grease a 13"x9" baking pan and spread half of mixture in bottom. Layer with half of pepperoni and mozzarella cheese; layer with remaining spaghetti mixture. Add remaining pepperoni and mozzarella cheese. Bake for 15 to 20 minutes at 350 degrees. Cut in squares and serve topped with sauce. Serves 6 to 8.

It's a comfort to always find pasta in the cupboard
and garlic and parsley in the garden.

–Alice Waters

Family-style Casseroles

Down-Home Tuna Casserole
Karen Urfer
New Philadelphia, OH

My family loves this creamy casserole! As the parents of two young children, my husband and I believe in the importance of sharing meals together. When I serve this casserole, everyone races to the table where we can sit as a family and share our blessings.

8-oz. pkg. egg noodles,
   uncooked
2 T. butter
1 c. celery, chopped
1/4 c. onion, chopped
10-3/4 oz. can cream of
   mushroom soup
2 T. all-purpose flour

3/4 c. milk
1/4 t. pepper
1/4 t. dried thyme
9-1/4 oz. can tuna, drained
   and flaked
1 stack round, buttery crackers,
   crushed
1/4 c. grated Parmesan cheese

Cook noodles according to package directions; drain and add to a 1-1/2 quart casserole dish. In a saucepan, melt butter; cook celery and onion until tender. Add to noodles. In a separate bowl, blend soup, flour, milk, pepper and thyme. Blend well and add tuna. Combine with noodles and mix well. Combine cracker crumbs with Parmesan cheese and sprinkle over top. Bake at 350 degrees for 25 minutes. Serves 6.

Hang an old-fashioned red, white and blue bunting over your door!

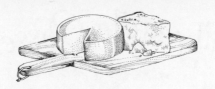

Sour Cream Enchiladas

Pam Hilton
Centerburg, OH

Always a favorite when served with Spanish rice or beans!

2 10-3/4 oz. cans cream of chicken soup
1 c. sour cream
2 c. shredded sharp Cheddar cheese
4-1/2 oz. can chopped green chiles, undrained

1/2 c. onion, diced
2 T. picante sauce
2 doz. corn tortillas
Garnish: shredded lettuce; additional shredded cheese and sour cream

Combine all ingredients except tortillas and garnish in a large saucepan. Cook and stir over low heat until cheese melts. Soften tortillas in very hot oil in a frying pan, for a few seconds on each side. Drain on paper towels. Spoon 2 tablespoons of soup mixture onto a tortilla, roll, and place in a 13"x9" baking pan. Continue with remaining tortillas. Pour remaining soup mixture over rolled tortillas and bake at 350 degrees for 25 to 30 minutes. Top with more cheese just before serving. Serve with shredded lettuce and sour cream. Serves 8.

Casserole: just another word for leftovers!

–Vinnie Tonellli

Mary's Noodle Bake

Mary Baker
Bayonet Point, FL

An easy casserole to prepare and perfect to share with neighbors.

16-oz. pkg. wide egg noodles,
   uncooked
1-1/2 lb. ground beef
4 onions, chopped
1 lb. sliced mushrooms
4 stalks celery, chopped

1 green pepper, chopped
2 T. butter
3 10-3/4 oz. cans tomato soup
juice of 1/2 lemon
1 lb. shredded sharp Cheddar
   cheese

Cook noodles according to package directions, drain and set aside.
Brown the ground beef and drain. Sauté the onions, mushrooms,
celery and green pepper in butter. Add beef mixture to a 3-quart
casserole dish; add remaining ingredients and fold in noodles. Bake
at 350 degrees for one hour or until bubbly. Serves 10.

*Search flea markets for primitive herb drying racks
with swinging arms...perfect for displaying
your homepsun kitchen towels!*

Old-Fashioned Pork Chop Bake

Sue Martin
Delaware, OH

An easy one-dish recipe that we make ahead of time, refrigerate and put in the oven before our family arrives for dinner.

salt and pepper to taste
6 pork chops
3/4 c. onion, thinly sliced
3/4 c. quick-cooking rice,
   uncooked

1 green pepper, sliced into rings
28-oz. can peeled whole
   tomatoes, undrained
15-oz. can tomato sauce

Lightly salt and pepper both sides of each pork chop. Arrange in a single layer in a lightly greased 13"x9" baking pan. Place one onion slice and 2 tablespoons of rice on each pork chop. Add one green pepper ring on top of each rice-topped pork chop. In a mixing bowl, combine undrained tomatoes and tomato sauce. Pour over pork chops, covering all rice. Cover and bake at 350 degrees for 1-1/2 hours. Serves 4 to 6.

Add a drawstring to old feed and sugar sacks and hang on a peg in the laundry room...great for sorting clothes!

Chicken & Green Bean Bake

Donna Lewis
Bellflower, CA

Perfect for a busy family...a quick recipe for your slow cooker!

2 to 3 boneless, skinless
   chicken breasts
salt, pepper and garlic powder
   to taste
10-3/4 oz. can cream of
   mushroom soup

1/2 c. milk
14-1/2 oz. can green beans,
   drained
2.8-oz. can French fried onions

Place chicken breasts in a 4-quart slow cooker. Season with salt, pepper and garlic powder to taste. Cover and cook on high setting for 2 to 3 hours, until chicken is done. Drain off any liquid; return chicken to pot. Add mushroom soup, milk and green beans. Cover mixture with onions. Sprinkle with pepper. Cover and cook 30 minutes longer. Serves 2 to 3.

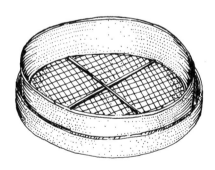

After a good dinner, one can forgive anybody,
even one's own relatives.

–Oscar Wilde

Family Night Noodle Bake

LaRayne Cummons
Lakeview, OH

Set aside one night each week to spend just with family...go for a walk, play games or read a favorite book. This quick & easy casserole will let you spend more time together!

2 c. wide egg noodles, uncooked
1 lb. ground beef
1/2 lb. ground pork
1/2 c. plus 2 T. butter, divided
2/3 c. onion, chopped
2 10-3/4 oz. cans tomato soup
3-oz. pkg. cream cheese, cubed
2 T. sugar
1-1/2 T. Worcestershire sauce
1 t. salt
1/4 t. pepper
1 c. corn flake cereal, crushed

Cook noodles according to package directions; set aside. In a large skillet, combine meats and brown lightly in butter. Add onion and cook until tender, but not brown. Add soup, cheese, sugar, Worcestershire sauce and seasonings. Simmer for 15 minutes. Place noodles in a buttered 11"x7" baking pan. Pour sauce over noodles. Mix cereal with remaining butter, melted, and sprinkle over the top. Bake at 350 degrees for 20 minutes, or until heated through. Serves 8.

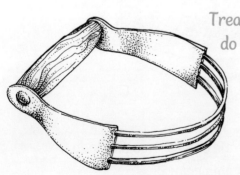

Treat your friends as you
do your pictures, and place them
in their best light.

–Jennie Jerome Churchill

Reuben Casserole

Phyllis Laughrey
Mount Vernon, OH

A favorite sandwich turned into a casserole!

2 16-oz. can sauerkraut,
   drained
2 12-oz. cans corned beef,
   crumbled
4 c. shredded Swiss cheese

1 c. mayonnaise
1 c. Thousand Island salad
   dressing
4 T. butter, melted
1/2 c. rye bread crumbs

In a 13"x9" baking pan, layer sauerkraut, corned beef and cheese. Set aside while preparing sauce. Mix mayonnaise and dressing together; pour over casserole mixture. Mix together butter and bread crumbs. Sprinkle generously over all. Bake at 375 degrees for 30 minutes. Makes 6 to 8 servings.

Display vintage linens, delicate lace or embroidered pillowcases on an antique quilt rack.

Chicken & Biscuits

Laura Fenneman
Lima, OH

Serve with a tall glass of milk and a crisp salad; delicious!

16-oz. pkg. frozen mixed
  vegetables
10-3/4 oz. can cream of
  chicken soup
8-oz. can chopped chicken
1 c. tomatoes, chopped

1-1/2 c. shredded Cheddar
  cheese, divided
1-1/2 c. milk, divided
1-1/2 c. biscuit baking mix
2.8-oz can French fried onions,
  divided

Cook vegetables according to package directions; drain. Combine vegetables, soup, chicken, tomatoes, one cup cheese and 3/4 cup milk. Spread in a greased 12"x8" baking pan. Cover and bake at 375 degrees for 15 minutes. Combine biscuit mix, 3/4 cup milk and 1/2 can onions. Mix thoroughly. Drop by spoonfuls to form 6 biscuits around edge of casserole. Bake, uncovered, until biscuits are light brown. Top with remaining cheese and onions. Bake until cheese is completely melted and onions are toasted. Makes 4 to 6 servings.

In the childhood memories of
every good cook, there's a large
kitchen, a warm stove,
a simmering pot and a Mom.

–Barbara Costikyan

Family-style Casseroles

Ruth's Rice Casserole

Dorothy Baldauf
Crystal Lake, IL

A recipe shared with me by a very dear friend.
This recipe can be served with beef, chicken or ham.

6 T. margarine
1 c. long-cooking rice, uncooked
3/4 c. onion, diced
3/4 c. green pepper, diced

4-oz. can mushroom stems and
   pieces, drained
10-3/4 oz. can chicken and
   rice soup
1-1/4 c. water

Melt margarine in a frying pan. Add rice; cook and stir until rice is brown. Add onion, green pepper and mushrooms, cooking until almost browned. Pour into a buttered 2-1/2 quart casserole dish; add chicken soup and water. Cover casserole and bake for 60 to 70 minutes at 350 degrees. Serves 4 to 6.

Spread a small coverlet on a child-size chair. Add a tin candle pan of wooden apples or dried oranges for a simple welcome.

Turkey Casserole

Anne Marie Wherthey
Tulsa, OK

My family enjoys this dish because it's so tasty, I enjoy it because it's easy to prepare!

1/2 c. celery, diced
1/2 c. onion, diced
2 T. butter
2 c. cooked turkey, diced
1/2 c. black olives, sliced

1/2 c. chicken broth
10-3/4 oz. can cream of
  chicken soup
1 c. Italian-style croutons
cooked rice or wide noodles

Sauté celery and onion in butter; add turkey and olives. Combine broth with soup and blend with turkey mixture. Add additional broth if needed to thin mixture. It should not be thick, but resemble soup. Pour into a buttered one-quart casserole dish. Top with croutons and bake at 375 degrees for 30 minutes. Serve over rice or wide noodles. Serves 6.

Home is heaven for beginners.

–Charles H. Parkhurst

Southwestern Chicken

Joanne West
Beavercreek, OH

Great for family reunions or neighborhood block parties!

1 t. salt
1/2 t. pepper
1/4 t. garlic powder
1-1/2 lbs. boneless, skinless
  chicken breasts, cubed
1/4 c. butter
1 c. fresh cilantro leaves,
  finely chopped

3-1/2 c. broccoli flowerets
1 lb. pasteurized process cheese,
  diced
10-oz. can diced tomatoes with
  green chiles
4 c. cooked rice
Garnish: sour cream

Combine salt, pepper and garlic powder well and sprinkle evenly over chicken. Heat butter in a large skillet; stir in cilantro and chicken. Cook for 10 minutes, stirring occasionally. Add broccoli; continue cooking until broccoli is tender and chicken juices run clear. Remove from heat and set aside. Combine cheese, tomatoes and green chiles in a saucepan and cook over low heat until cheese melts. Remove from heat and set aside. Spoon rice into a greased 2-1/2 quart casserole; top with chicken mixture. Pour cheese mixture over chicken. Cover and bake at 350 degrees for 25 to 30 minutes. Garnish with sour cream. Serves 6 to 8.

A man travels the world over in search of what he needs and returns home to find it.

−George Moore

Scalloped Tomato Casserole

Ann Magner
New Port Richey, FL

This recipe is over 100 years old!

6 slices bacon, diced
1/2 c. celery, chopped
1/2 c. onion, chopped
28-oz. can whole tomatoes,
    undrained and broken up
4 slices bread, torn into pieces
1 T. brown sugar, packed

1/2 t. salt
1/2 t. dried summer savory
    or thyme
1/4 t. pepper
2 T. butter, sliced
2 T. grated Parmesan cheese

In a large skillet, cook bacon until crisp. Set aside bacon; drain all but 2 tablespoons of drippings. Stir in celery and onion; sauté until tender. Add remaining ingredients except butter and cheese; blend well. Place mixture into a lightly oiled 1-1/2 quart casserole dish. Dot with butter and sprinkle with cheese. Bake for 30 minutes at 350 degrees. Serves 6.

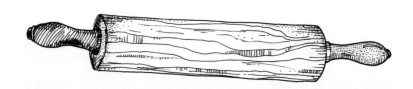

Recall it as often as you wish, a happy memory never wears out.

– Libbie Fudim

Apple Valley Squash Casserole

Rebecca Norris
Apple Valley, MN

As far as our family knows, my grandmother created this recipe...without any specific measurements!

4 to 5 yellow squash, chopped	1 egg, beaten
2 T. butter	1/4 lb. saltine crackers, crushed
1/2 c. sugar	nutmeg and pepper to taste

Cover squash with water in a medium saucepan and cook until tender. Drain. Add butter to squash in pan and mash with a potato masher until fairly smooth. Add sugar and egg; mix. Add enough cracker crumbs to make mix about the consistency of cornbread batter. Pour into a buttered 9" pie plate; sprinkle with nutmeg and pepper. Bake at 350 degrees for about 25 minutes or until lightly brown on top and around edges. Serves 6.

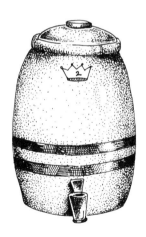

A collection of sterling-silver tea balls is beautiful nestled in an old porcelain bowl.

Chicken King Casserole

Wendy Lee Paffenroth
Pine Island, NY

We serve this with a salad or coleslaw and warm bread. It's quick, great for leftover chicken and gone in one sitting...my family loves it!

6 boneless, skinless chicken
  breasts
4 oz. bowtie pasta, uncooked
10-3/4 oz. can cream of
  broccoli soup
10-3/4 oz. can creamy chicken
  mushroom soup
4-oz. can mushroom stems and
  pieces, drained and rinsed
1/2 c. milk

16-oz. container sour cream
1 c. frozen peas
1 sleeve saltine crackers,
  crushed
2 T. butter, melted
1/4 t. dried parsley
1/4 t. garlic powder
1/4 t. celery seed
1/4 t. salt

Boil chicken in water until cooked through. Cut up and place in a large mixing bowl; set aside. Cook pasta according to package directions, drain and rinse. In a medium mixing bowl, whisk together soups, mushrooms, milk, sour cream and peas. Combine crackers and butter well. Spread 3/4 of the cracker mixture over the bottom of a 13"x9" baking dish. Layer chicken, pasta and spices. Pour soup mixture over pasta layer, sprinkle with reserved cracker mixture. Bake at 350 degrees for 30 to 40 minutes or until heated through. Serves 6.

A dog wags its tail with its heart.

—Martin Buxbaum

Hometown
Main Dishes

I can still recall my mother telling me, "Don't get your Sunday clothes dirty, we'll be leaving any minute!" I knew if I behaved, I could bring a friend home for dinner and we could play all afternoon. After services were over, the members would visit outside awhile and then go home.

My friend and I would sit on the back steps playing jacks and getting more and more hungry by the minute. After what seemed like forever, Mom would call us in for dinner!

We'd take our places at the table and Dad would say the blessing. We'd then eagerly pass around plates of fried chicken, mashed potatoes and gravy, corn on the cob, warm rolls and icy lemonade. Sunday dinner was a special occasion at our house...everyone talking and laughing at the same time.

After dinner my friend and I would play outside, swing in the tree or take a bike ride, reluctant for the day to end.

Country Pork Chops

Crystal Lappie
Worthington, OH

This recipe came from my kitchen creativity...a little of this and a little of that! It's my favorite recipe because it's so simple to prepare and delicious! The meat is so tender it can be cut with a fork.

4 to 6 pork chops   1/2 c. butter, melted
6-oz. pkg. herb stuffing mix

Place pork chops in a shallow 13"x9" baking pan. Bake, uncovered, at 350 degrees for one hour. Prepare the herb stuffing mix according to the box directions. Remove cooked pork chops from the oven and layer the stuffing mix on each pork chop. Drizzle with melted butter. Return to oven for an additional 15 to 20 minutes. Serves 4 to 6.

Use it up, wear it out; make it do, or do without.

–New England Proverb

One-Pot Supper

Wendy Lee Paffenroth
Pine Island, NY

A favorite in our family and the whole meal can be prepared in less than 30 minutes! We like it best served with salad and corn muffins.

8-oz. pkg. egg noodles,
    uncooked
1-1/2 lbs. ground beef
1/2 c. onion, chopped
10 1/2-oz. can cream of
    mushroom soup
3/4 c. milk

1/8 t. pepper
1 t. fresh parsley, chopped
8-oz. pkg. light cream cheese,
    cubed
16-oz. can whole-kernel corn,
    drained and rinsed

Cook egg noodles according to package directions; set aside. In a heavy Dutch oven, brown beef with onion. Drain. Mix in mushroom soup and milk; stir well until blended. Add pepper, parsley and cream cheese. Keep stirring until the cream cheese is melted. Add corn. When ready to serve, spoon over egg noodles. Serves 4.

Wisdom doesn't necessarily come with age. Sometimes age just shows up all by itself.

—Tom Wilson

Double-Crust Chicken Pot Pie, page 138

Apple-Stuffed French Toast,
page 18

Farmhouse Sausage Gravy, page 21

Tomato Bisque, page 58

Sunflower Strawberry Salad, page 84

Sloppy Joes, page 129

Meatloaf, page 139

Garlic Smashed Potatoes, page 179

Escalloped Corn, page 171

Buttermilk Biscuits, page 36

German Potato Salad, page 157

Corn Fritters, page 49

Shrimp with Garlic, page 104

Country Chicken Stew, page 53

Old-Fashioned Meatballs, page 134

Pepper Steak, page 145

Shepherd's Pie, page 103

Farmstead Split Pea Soup, page 55

Peanut Butter Fudge, page 217

Texas Sheet Cake, page 206

Fresh Peach Pie, page 200

Sloppy Joes

Pat Decker
N. Muskegon, MI

Our family still thinks these are the best...tangy, rather than spicy.

1 lb. ground beef
10-3/4 oz. can tomato soup
1/2 green pepper, diced
2 T. vinegar

1 t. sugar
1/2 c. onion, diced
2 T. Worcestershire sauce
sandwich buns, split

Brown ground beef in a medium saucepan and drain. Add remaining ingredients to beef. Simmer over low heat for 30 to 60 minutes, until heated through. Serve on buns. Makes 6 sandwiches.

Colonial Dinner

Kendra Landry
Mancelonia, MI

An old-fashioned family dinner.

6 pork chops
3 T. oil
1 c. celery, chopped
1 orange, thinly sliced

2 c. cranberries, chopped
1/4 c. sugar
1/4 c. brown sugar, packed
salt and pepper to taste

Sauté pork chops in oil until browned. Remove from skillet and sauté celery and orange slices for 5 to 10 minutes. Return pork chops to pan; top with cranberries, sugars, salt and pepper. Cover and simmer 30 minutes. Turn pork chops and continue to simmer an additional 30 minutes. Serves 4 to 6.

*Frame the pages of an old vintage scrapbook
to make a wonderful wall display!*

Pork & Sauerkraut Supper

Karen Mohn
Bethel, PA

We love this recipe because it's wonderful when we combine it with mashed potatoes and fresh ingredients grown on our farm!

6 country-style pork ribs
2 T. oil
3/4 c. onion, diced
1 c. apple juice, divided

32-oz. pkg. sauerkraut, drained
2 apples, cored and diced
2 t. brown sugar, packed
salt and pepper to taste

Brown pork in oil. Remove from pan. Cook onion in drippings until tender. Stir in 1/4 cup apple juice. In a large covered roaster, combine onion, drippings, sauerkraut, apples, sugar and remaining apple juice. Tuck pork into kraut and sprinkle with salt and pepper. Cover and bake at 350 degrees for 2 hours, basting occasionally. Serves 3 to 4.

A stack of vintage luggage found in an old attic, can make a terrific end table or nightstand.

Main Dishes

Smothered Steak

Stephanie Quincy
Iola, KS

An old-fashioned recipe...great with roasted corn!

3/4 c. milk, divided
1/2 c. all-purpose flour
4 beef round steaks, tenderized
4 T. oil

1/2 c. yellow onion, diced
10-3/4 oz. can cream of
   mushroom soup
salt and pepper to taste

Place 1/4 cup milk and flour in separate bowls. Dip steak into milk then dredge in flour on both sides. Brown steaks in oil on both sides; place in a 3-quart casserole dish. Sauté onion until tender; add soup and remaining milk. Simmer until gravy thickens and pour over steak. Bake, covered, for 45 minutes at 350 degrees. Remove lid and bake an additional 15 minutes. Serves 4.

Nobody can do for little children
what grandparents do.
Grandparents sort of sprinkle
stardust over the lives
of little children.

–Alex Haley

Grandma's Yankee Fried Chicken

Natalie Giberson
Keflavik, Iceland

A great old recipe that's been handed down for years!

6 boneless, skinless chicken
   breasts
3 eggs, beaten

1/2 c. butter
1-1/2 c. dry bread crumbs

Simmer chicken in water until juices run clear when pierced with a fork. Set aside to cool. Beat eggs in a bowl. Set aside. In a large skillet, melt butter over low heat. Cut chicken breasts into several pieces and dip in egg mixture; roll in bread crumbs. Fry chicken in butter, turning every few minutes until golden brown. Place on plate with paper towel to remove any excess butter. Serves 6.

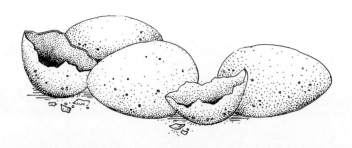

That is the best...to laugh with someone because
you both think the same things are funny.

– Gloria Vanderbilt

Easy Stroganoff

Kathy Williamson
Delaware, OH

Quick to make for a family on the go!

1 lb. ground beef	1-1/4 c. hot water
1/2 c. onion, chopped	8-oz. container sour cream
10-3/4 oz. can cream of	cooked rice or noodles
chicken soup	

Brown ground beef and onion; drain. Combine soup and hot water; add to beef mixture. Simmer over low heat for one hour, until most of the liquid has cooked off. Just before serving, add sour cream. Serve over prepared rice or noodles. Makes 4 servings.

For the laughter of children who fumble barefooted and bareheaded in the summer grass...our prayer of thanks.

–Carl Sandburg

Old-Fashioned Meatballs

Wendy Lee Paffenroth
Pine Island, NY

These are terrific because you can double the recipe and freeze them to use later. I wear a new pair of plastic cleaning gloves to roll the meatballs...less cleanup!

2 lbs. ground beef round
2 eggs, beaten
2 t. Worcestershire sauce
1/4 c. catsup
1/4 c. onion, minced

1 t. dried oregano
1/8 t. pepper
2 c. Italian-seasoned dry
   bread crumbs

Combine all ingredients in a large bowl and mix well. Roll into meatballs. Place evenly on a baking sheet and bake at 325 degrees for about 30 minutes; drain. Cool and freeze in zipping freezer bags for future meals. Serves 8.

My father didn't tell me how to live; he lived,
and let me watch him do it.

–Clarence Budington Kelland

Mom's Spaghetti Sauce

Jeannine Johnson-Tatum
Wauchula, FL

Every time I smell this sauce cooking, I can't help but think of Mom's dedication and determination to make everything she does the absolute best! This recipe is filled with Mom's timeless love!

1/2 c. onion, diced
3 cloves garlic, chopped
1 T. butter
3 14-1/2 oz. cans diced
    tomatoes
3 6-oz. cans tomato paste
2 c. water
2 T. sugar
1/4 t. salt

1/2 t. pepper
1/2 t. dried basil
1/2 t. dried oregano
1/2 t. garlic powder
1/2 t. dried thyme
1 t. Italian seasoning
2 bay leaves
1 T. dried parsley
3 T. olive oil

Sauté onion and garlic in butter. Process tomatoes and tomato paste in a blender until smooth. Combine with onion and garlic; spoon into a slow cooker. Gradually add the remaining ingredients. Cover and cook on high for about 3 hours, stirring occasionally. Discard bay leaves. Serves 10 to 12.

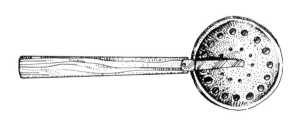

Old yelloware bowls are beautiful filled with apples, pomegranates, dried oranges, leaves or acorns.

Country Roast

Sandy Peterson
Glen Ellyn, IL

An easy roast to prepare and the gravy is wonderful served over mashed potatoes!

3-lb. beef chuck roast
1 pkg. onion soup mix
10-3/4 oz. can cream of
   mushroom soup

1/2 to 3/4 c. milk

Place roast on heavy-duty aluminum foil. Sprinkle dry soup mix over roast; spread mushroom soup over top. Wrap tightly with foil. Bake at 325 degrees in a roasting pan for 3-1/2 hours. To prepare gravy, add milk to pan drippings; stir well and heat through. Serves 4 to 5.

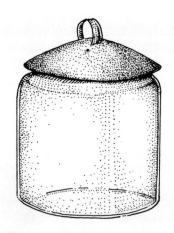

A sister is a gift to the heart, a friend to the spirit,
a golden thread to the meaning of life.

−Anonymous

Main Dishes

Chicken & Dumplings

Megan Pepping
Coshocton, OH

You can't go wrong with this homestyle dish...it's guaranteed
to stick to your ribs!

4 lbs. chicken breasts
2 carrots, peeled and thinly
 sliced
2 celery stalks, thinly sliced
1 onion, chopped

1/2 t. dried rosemary
1-1/2 t. dried thyme
2 t. salt
1/2 t. pepper

Place chicken breasts in a large stockpot. Cover with water. Add carrots, celery, onion, rosemary, thyme, salt and pepper. Bring to a boil. Reduce to a simmer. Cook for 30 to 45 minutes, until juices run clear when chicken is pierced. Remove from pot and shred. Return to broth. Drop dumpling dough by spoonfuls on top of boiling chicken mixture. Cover and steam for 20 minutes without lifting the lid. Don't even peek! Serves 6 to 8.

Dumplings:

2 c. all-purpose flour
3 t. baking powder
1 t. salt

2 T. fresh parsley, minced
4 T. shortening
3/4 to 1 c. milk

Combine flour, baking powder, salt and parsley in a bowl. Cut in shortening until mixture resembles coarse meal. Add milk and stir briefly with a fork. If necessary, add additional milk to make dough hold together.

When I was younger, I could remember anything;
whether it happened or not.

– Mark Twain

Double-Crust Chicken Pot Pie

Margaret McNeil
Memphis, TN

Delicious, tender chicken pot pie...
a true comfort food that's easy to prepare.

2 9-inch refrigerated pie crusts
5-oz. can boneless chicken in
  broth, undrained, chopped
16-oz. can mixed vegetables,
  drained

10-3/4 oz. can cream of chicken
  soup
1/2 t. celery flakes
1/4 t. pepper
1/4 t. poultry seasoning

Place one refrigerated pie crust into a 9" pie plate according to package directions; do not bake. Combine remaining ingredients together and spoon into pie crust. Place second crust on top; fold edges under and flute. Cut slits in top. Bake at 400 degrees for 45 to 50 minutes. Let stand 10 minutes before serving. Serves 6.

There's nothing half so pleasant
as coming home again.

– Margaret Sangster

Meatloaf

Dee Rogers
S. Charleston, WV

Family-style meatloaf with a special sauce.

1-1/2 lbs. lean ground beef
1 c. tomato juice
3/4 c. quick-cooking oats,
    uncooked
1 egg or 2 egg whites, beaten

1/4 c. onion, chopped
1/4 c. green pepper, chopped
1/2 t. salt
1/4 t. pepper

Combine all ingredients and mix lightly. Press into 8"x4" loaf pan. Spoon piquant sauce over the meatloaf. Bake at 350 degrees for one hour. Drain and let stand for 5 minutes. Serves 6.

Piquant Sauce:

3 T. brown sugar, packed
1/4 c. catsup

1/4 t. nutmeg
1 t. dry mustard

Mix together all ingredients.

Cut a primitive star shape from an old piece of wood and paint it an old-fashioned color. When dry, twine a length of grapevine around and hang on your barn or milkhouse door!

Barbecued Pork Chops

Mary Marshall
Johnstown, PA.

Of all my mom's great meals, this was her best. When I make her
recipe for my family and smell that wonderful aroma, I can
close my eyes and see her face.

8 pork chops
3 T. oil
1/2 c. catsup
1 t. salt
1 t. celery seed

1/2 t. nutmeg
1/3 c. vinegar
1 c. water
1 bay leaf

Brown chops in hot oil. Combine remaining ingredients and pour over
pork chops. Cover and bake at 325 degrees for 1-1/2 hours. Discard
bay leaf. Serves 8.

Display old-fashioned kitchen utensils in
a favoite basket lined with homespun.

Mom's Lazy Lasagna

Kimberly Nuttall
San Marcos, CA

Making this lasagna recipe always brings to mind special occasions in my home.

1 lb. ground beef
2 28-oz. cans crushed tomatoes
8-oz. can tomato sauce
1/4 t. garlic salt
1 env. spaghetti sauce mix
1 c. ricotta or cottage cheese

1 egg, beaten
1/2 c. grated Parmesan cheese
8-oz. pkg. lasagna noodles, uncooked
6-oz. pkg. shredded mozzarella cheese

Brown beaf in a large saucepan; drain. Add tomatoes with juice, tomato sauce, garlic salt and sauce mix. Bring to a boil and simmer for 10 minutes. In a small bowl, mix ricotta or cottage cheese, egg and Parmesan cheese. Spread a little of the beef sauce in bottom of a 13"x9" baking pan and alternate layers as follows: noodles, 1/3 of beef sauce, half of cheese mixture. Repeat and then top with remaining sauce. Sprinkle mozzarella cheese on top and cover with aluminum foil. Bake at 350 degrees for one hour or until noodles are tender. Let stand 10 minutes before cutting. Serves 8 to 10.

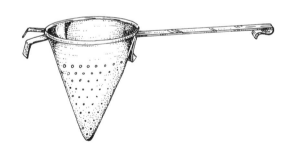

Life is a combination of magic and pasta.

—Federico Fellini

Grandma's Stuffed Cabbage

Karen Pungaew
Riverside, CA

*This recipe is special to me because it belongs to my Grandma Ponto.
She was not only the best grandma, but she was also the best cook.
When we were little we would cook all sorts of wonderful things, but
the best recipe she had was stuffed cabbage. We always made
it at Christmastime.*

1/2 c. onion, diced	1 c. long-cooking rice, uncooked
2 T. oil	4-lb. head cabbage
2 lbs. pork shoulder, ground	14-oz. can sauerkraut, divided
salt and pepper to taste	1 pt. tomatoes, chopped

Sauté onion in oil; add pork and seasonings. Rinse rice thoroughly and
add to pork mixture. Cut out the center core of the cabbage head and
put cabbage in boiling water. Simmer cabbage just until leaves begin
to wilt. Remove leaves and set aside. Remove the vein in the center of
the leaves, without cutting through the leaves. Spoon 2 tablespoons
of meat mixture on each leaf. Roll up filled leaves, pushing both ends
in tightly. Repeat with remaining wilted cabbage leaves. Any remaining
cabbage can be chopped and lined inside the bottom of a Dutch oven.
On top, layer 1/2 of the sauerkraut, stuffed cabbage rolls and remaining
sauerkraut. Cover with tomatoes; add enough water to cover all. Bring
to a boil, then reduce heat to low. Simmer for 15 minutes. Makes
20 cabbage rolls.

Memory is more indelible than ink.

−Anita Loos

Chicken Cacciatora

Mildred Panfile
Bayville, NJ

When we were on vacation in Long Island, New York, a wonderful Italian restaurant served this dish and I just had to learn how to make it! By trial and error, I did learn and now I've been making it for our family for many years.

4 lbs. chicken, cut into pieces
1/2 c. all-purpose flour
1 t. salt
1 t. pepper
1/2 c. oil
1/4 c. onion, chopped
2 cloves garlic, finely chopped
1/2 c. carrots, peeled and
    chopped

1 T. dried parsley
1 bay leaf
1 t. dried basil
4 c. plum tomatoes, chopped
    and drained
1/4 c. red or white wine
cooked rice or angel hair pasta

Dredge chicken in flour; sprinkle with salt and pepper and brown in hot oil until golden brown on all sides. Place in a covered dish and keep warm. Brown onion, garlic, carrots, parsley, bay leaf and basil in oil left in pan. Add tomatoes to onion mixture. Bring to a boil. Add chicken and wine; simmer 30 minutes or until chicken is tender. Discard bay leaf. Serve with prepared rice or angel hair pasta. Serves 4 to 6.

Sunflowers tucked into cobalt blue jars make a colorful display on your windowsill!

143

Farm-Fresh Spinach Quiche

Margaret Sloan
Westerville, OH

Use farm-fresh eggs for this recipe!

9-inch refrigerated pie crust
8 slices bacon, crisply cooked
   and crumbled
1/2 lb. shredded Monterey Jack
   cheese

3 eggs, beaten
1-1/2 c. milk
1 T. all-purpose flour
10-oz. pkg. frozen spinach,
   thawed and drained

Lay pie crust in a 9" pie plate. Add 4 slices of crumbled bacon to bottom of pie crust. Mix cheese, eggs, milk, flour and spinach together. Spoon over crust. Sprinkle remaining crumbled bacon on top. Bake at 350 degrees for one hour or until center is set. Cut into wedges. Serves 4 to 6.

Old-fashioned canning jars make perfect canisters
for your country kitchen!

Main Dishes

Pepper Steak

Mary Alice Foster
Reynoldsburg, OH

This wonderful recipe brings back such lovely memories! Memories of my brothers and sisters and our father coming in from the barn, stomping the snow off his boots, and our mother who had to stretch pennies into dollars. We were Depression Era kids, but the warmth and love in our home made us rich beyond belief. We always teased our father that he came in early from the barn when he knew we were having this dish!

1 lb. beef round steak, fat trimmed	1/8 t. pepper
1 T. oil	14-1/2 oz. can stewed tomatoes
1/4 c. onion, chopped	1 green pepper, cut into strips
1 clove garlic, minced	1/4 c. cold water
1 cube beef bouillon	2 T. cornstarch
3/4 c. boiling water	2 t. soy sauce
	cooked rice or noodles

Cut round steak into 2-inch strips. Add oil to skillet and brown beef for 10 minutes. Add onion and garlic; cook for 3 to 4 minutes. Dissolve bouillon cube in boiling water and pour into skillet. Sprinkle beef with pepper. Cover and simmer for 35 to 40 minutes, or until beef is tender. Add tomatoes and green pepper; cover and simmer for 10 minutes. Combine cold water, cornstarch and soy sauce. Stir into skillet. Bring to a boil, and stir for 2 minutes. Serve over rice or noodles. Serves 4 to 6.

There is no spectacle on earth more appealing than that of a beautiful woman in the act of cooking dinner for someone she loves.

– Thomas Wolfe

Deep-Dish Vegetable Pie

Vickie
Gooseberry Patch

Cut this pie into wedges and serve warm...delicious!

Crust:

1 pkg. active dry yeast
2/3 c. warm water
2 c. all-purpose flour, divided
1/2 c. corn chips, finely crushed

1 T. sugar
2 t. onion, finely chopped
3/4 t. salt
2 T. oil

In a small bowl, dissolve yeast in water; set side. In another bowl, combine one cup flour, corn chips, sugar, onion and salt; stir until well blended. Add yeast mixture and oil to flour mixture. Stir until smooth. Add remaining flour; stirring until well blended. Roll dough out to a 13-inch diameter circle on a lightly floured surface. Press dough into the bottom and sides of a well-greased 9" springform pan. Cover with a cloth and let rise for 10 minutes. Pierce bottom of crust with a fork. Bake at 375 degrees for 25 to 30 minutes until golden brown.

Filling:

1 T. oil
1 T. butter
3 c. fresh broccoli flowerets
3 c. cabbage, shredded
2 c. zucchini squash, thinly
   sliced
3 onions, chopped
1-1/2 c. carrots, peeled
   and sliced

1 t. salt
1/2 t. pepper
1/4 t. garlic powder
1/4 t. chili powder
1-1/2 c. shredded sharp
   Cheddar cheese

In a large skillet, heat oil and butter over medium heat. Add remaining ingredients except cheese, stirring constantly. Cook until vegetables are crisp-tender. Spoon over warm crust and sprinkle with cheese. Bake at 375 degrees for 8 to 10 minutes, or until cheese is melted. Cut into wedges. Serves 10.

Main Dishes

Beef Brisket with Ginger Gravy

Teri Lindquist
Gurnee, IL

The only difficult part of of making this recipe is waiting for it to be ready! We serve this on buns for easy sandwiches or with mashed potatoes and carrots for dinner.

2 pkgs. onion soup mix
2 c. water
8 to 10-lb. beef brisket

12-oz. bottle chili sauce
10 gingersnap cookies

Pour onion soup mix into bottom of a large roasting pan. Pour in water and stir to combine. Place brisket into pan and cover meat with chili sauce. Break cookies into pieces and sprinkle around brisket. Cover tightly and bake at 350 degrees for 1-1/2 hours. Check occasionally and add more water if necessary. Remove brisket from pan and thinly slice. Return sliced beef to pan and spoon sauce over top. Cover and bake another hour. Then turn heat down to 250 degrees and bake another 2 to 3 hours, until very tender. Serves 8 to 10.

Vintage toy trucks make fun utensil or
napkin holders.

Stuffed Peppers

Dorothy Foor
Jeromesville, OH

A homestyle dish with a twist.

4 green peppers	1 jalapeño pepper, chopped
4 slices bacon, cut into	1-1/4 t. chili powder
2-inch pieces	1-1/4 t. ground cumin
1 c. green onions, chopped	1/2 t. salt
2 c. frozen corn kernels, thawed	1 c. shredded Monterey Jack
1/4 c. pimentos, chopped	cheese, divided
3 T. fresh cilantro, chopped	1/4 c. tortilla chips, crushed

Slice 1/2 inch off the top of each pepper; remove stem from top, chop and reserve. Remove seeds from peppers and rinse well with cool water. Blanch peppers 5 minutes in boiling water. Remove and set on paper towels. Cook bacon until crisp and set aside to drain, leaving 2 tablespoons bacon drippings in the skillet. Sauté chopped pepper in bacon drippings until soft. Stir in onions and sauté with peppers for 2 minutes. Add corn, pimentos, cilantro, jalapeño, chili powder, cumin and salt; cook and stir 3 minutes more. Remove from heat; stir in reserved bacon and 3/4 cup Monterey Jack cheese. Spoon an equal amount of corn mixture into peppers. Place peppers in an ungreased 1-1/2 quart casserole dish and bake, uncovered, at 350 degrees for 30 minutes. Toss crushed tortilla chips with the remaining cheese and place one tablespoon on top of each stuffed pepper. Continue to bake until cheese is melted. Serves 4.

Some wives do wonderful things with leftovers...
they throw them out!

–Anonymous

Swiss Steak

Betty Stout
Worthington, OH

If you have a busy family or a full day planned, make this hearty dish even easier! Brown the steak and place it in a slow cooker, top with the remaining ingredients and turn to the low setting. Enjoy a day at the park or beach and come home to a terrific meal in 8 to 10 hours!

1/4 c. all-purpose flour
1/2 t. salt
1/8 t. pepper
2-lb. beef round steak, cut into
   serving-size pieces
2 T. oil

28-oz. can whole tomatoes,
   undrained and broken up
1 stalk celery, chopped
3/4 c. onion, sliced
1 T. bottled steak sauce

In a shallow dish, combine flour, salt and pepper. Coat both sides of steak pieces with mixture. In a large skillet, brown steak in oil. Remove steak from pan; drain fat and return steak to skillet. Add remaining ingredients and bring to a boil. Reduce heat; cover and simmer for 1-1/2 to 2 hours, until tender. If desired, thicken gravy with additional flour dissolved in a small amount of water. Serves 6 to 8.

Show off your display of homespun kitchen towels in your favorite stoneware mixing bowl!

Chicken & Stuffing

Debbie Keady
Amsterdam, NY

You'll be asked for the recipe after friends taste this delicious dish!

2 to 4 boneless, skinless chicken
  breasts
10-3/4 oz. can cream of
  chicken soup
1/4 c. milk
1/4 c. chicken broth

6-oz. pkg. chicken-flavored
  stuffing mix
4 T. butter, melted
1/2 c. chicken broth
Garnish: grated Parmesan
  cheese

Place chicken breasts in a Dutch oven; cover with water and cook until juices run clear when pierced with a fork. Drain, reserving broth; set aside. Cut chicken in small pieces and place in a greased 1-1/2 quart casserole dish. Combine soup, milk and broth. Pour over chicken. Combine stuffing seasoning mix packet, butter and broth. Stir in dry stuffing and sprinkle on top of soup mixture. Cover and bake at 350 degrees for 30 minutes. Sprinkle with grated Parmesan cheese before serving. Serves 4 to 6.

After dinner sit awhile, after supper walk a mile.

– Anonymous

Layered Cabbage Rolls
Debbie Cummons-Parker
Lakeview, OH

The traditional meal we love, with a recipe that's half the work!

1 head cabbage, sliced or
    chopped
1-1/2 lbs. ground beef
1/2 lb. ground pork sausage
1/2 c. onion, chopped
1/4 c. green pepper, chopped
1 t. chili powder
1/4 t. garlic powder

1/2 t. salt
1/8 t. pepper
2/3 c. long-cooking rice,
    uncooked
2 10-3/4 oz. cans cream of
    tomato soup
2-1/2 c. water
2 T. brown sugar, packed

Lightly oil a 13"x9" glass baking pan. Do not use a metal pan. Layer cabbage in bottom of pan. Brown ground beef, sausage, onion and green pepper; drain. Add seasonings and rice to mixture; spread over cabbage. Mix together soup, water and brown sugar; pour over ingredients. Cover and bake at 350 degrees for 1-1/2 hours. Serves 6 to 8.

If six cooks followed the same recipe,
the finished dish would vary
six times.

–Theodora Fitzgibbon

Quick Chili Mac

Letty Lee Powers
Lakeview, OH

This is a quick, nutritious meal for the family on the go!

1 c. elbow macaroni, uncooked
1 green pepper, chopped
1 lg. onion, chopped
2 T. margarine
1 lb. ground beef

10-3/4 oz. can tomato soup
16-oz. can kidney beans
1/2 t. salt
1/2 t. chili powder

Prepare macaroni as directed on package. Drain and set aside. Sauté green pepper and onion in margarine until translucent. Add ground beef and brown. Add tomato soup, kidney beans, salt and chili powder. Simmer over low heat for 20 minutes. Add macaroni and heat through. Serves 4.

Old, rusty cookie cutters make whimsical windchimes outside your kitchen window!

Country Sides

Early in the morning, we'd walk across the dewy grass to the garden to see if any of the early vegetables were ready to pick. There was always something exciting about going between the rows and discovering a bounty of fresh vegetables!

We'd fill our baskets to overflowing and then head back to the farmhouse. Mom had set chairs under our old shade tree and we'd sit together and shell peas, snap beans or husk corn. We'd then gather our vegetables together and go to the summer kitchen, where they were quickly blanched and packed for the freezer.

We never picked so many that it became a chore, and many times friends or relatives were there to share the work. Afterwards we'd sit down together for dinner, sampling some of our freshly-picked vegetables...green beans and new potatoes, slices of bright red tomatoes and crisp homemade pickles. As the evening wore on, the song of the birds gave way to dancing fireflies and the sound of peepers. We'd watch and listen and grow sleepy.

Country Sides

Family-Style Baked Beans

Delores Berg
Selah, WA

A great side dish our family loves served with warm corn bread.

2 c. dried navy beans, rinsed and sorted
1-1/2 c. smoked ham, cubed
1/2 c. onion, chopped

1-1/2 c. brown sugar, packed
8-oz. can tomato sauce
1/2 t. salt
1/8 t. pepper

Soak beans overnight in cold water. In the mornng, drain; cover with fresh water. Simmer beans until tender, about one hour. Drain. Add beans, ham and onion to a bean pot. Combine brown sugar, tomato sauce and seasonings. Pour over beans. Add enough cold water to cover. Cover and bake at 300 degrees for 5-1/2 to 6 hours. Serves 8.

Simplicity is the essence
of happiness.

– Cedric Bledsoe

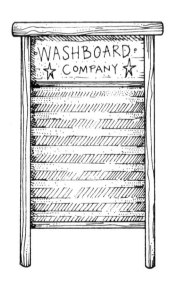

Ham & Cauliflower Au Gratin

Tiffany Moore
Grants Pass, OR

*One of my favorite recipes because I know that my kids will
eat their veggies without complaining!*

2 10-oz. pkgs. frozen
   cauliflower, thawed
   and drained
1-1/4 c. smoked ham, chopped
10-3/4 oz. can Cheddar
   cheese soup

1/4 c. milk
2/3 c. biscuit baking mix
2 T. butter
1/2 t. nutmeg
Optional: dried parsley
   and paprika

Arrange cauliflower in an ungreased 13"x9" baking pan. Sprinkle with
ham. Combine soup and milk; beat with an electric mixer until smooth.
Pour over ham. Mix remaining ingredients until crumbly. Sprinkle over
soup mixture. Sprinkle with parsley and paprika, if desired. Bake at
400 degrees until topping is golden brown, 20 to 25 minutes. Serves 8.

*Wrap a bundle of dried herbs from
your kichen garden in a vintage
handkerchief...a perfect hostess gift!*

Country Sides

German Potato Salad

Calla Andrews
Long Beach, CA

German Potato Salad was one of my first cooking successes as a new bride. My husband and his family raved over this recipe!

6 large new potatoes
10 slices bacon, chopped
1 red onion, finely chopped
4 t. all-purpose flour
1 T. sugar

salt and pepper
1/2 c. cider vinegar
1/2 c. water
1/4 c. fresh parsley, minced
1 t. celery seed

Steam potatoes until tender; cool and peel. Chop potatoes and transfer to a large bowl. Cook bacon in a heavy skillet over medium heat until crisp. Add onion; cook one minute. Stir in flour and sugar. Season with salt and pepper; stir. Mix vinegar and water; pour over bacon mixture. Stir until thickened. Pour over potatoes. Mix in parsley and celery seed. Makes 6 to 8 servings.

What small potatoes we all are,
compared with what we might be!

–Charles Dudley Warner

Cowboy Beans

Tambry Gardner
Delaware, OH

Great with grilled hamburgers or hot dogs and fresh corn on the cob!

1 lb. ground beef, browned and
    drained
16-oz. can baked beans
16-oz. can kidney beans
2 c. onions, chopped

3/4 c. brown sugar, packed
1 c. catsup
2 T. dry mustard
1/4 t. salt
2 t. vinegar

Mix all ingredients together in a crockpot. Cover and cook on high setting for one to 2 hours. until heated through. Serves 8 to 10.

Add a collection of birdhouses and pie birds to the shelves
of your kitchen cupboard.

Country Sides

Old-Fashioned Macaroni & Cheese
Kathy Schroeder
Riverside, CA

A wonderful comfort food, so smooth and creamy.

2 c. elbow macaroni, uncooked
2 T. shortening, melted
2 T. all-purpose flour
salt and pepper to taste

2-1/2 c. milk
3 c. shredded sharp Cheddar
   cheese, divided

Cook macaroni according to package instructions; drain. Mix together shortening and flour in a large saucepan over low heat. Add salt and pepper to taste. Gradually add milk, stirring constantly. Cook over medium heat just until it starts to boil and thicken. Add 2 cups Cheddar cheese and stir until smooth. Pour in macaroni; transfer to a greased 2-quart casserole dish. Top with remaining cheese and bake, uncovered, at 350 degrees for 30 minutes. Serves 8.

Many's the long night I've dreamed of cheese...toasted, mostly.

– Robert Louis Stevenson

Sweet Potato Casserole

Cindy Henderson
Greenville, SC

*This side dish has been a part of our meals for many years. My
mother used to make it each year for Christmas dinner; now we
gather at my house and I carry on the tradition. Whatever the reason
for the occasion, no meal is complete without this.*

3 c. sweet potatoes, mashed
1 c. sugar
1/2 t. salt
2 eggs, beaten

2-1/2 T. margarine, melted
1/2 c. milk
1 t. vanilla extract

Mix all ingredients together and pour into a greased 13"x9" baking
pan. Sprinkle topping over sweet potatoes in baking pan. Bake at
350 degrees for 30 to 35 minutes, until brown sugar melts. Recipe
may be doubled or tripled. Serves 8.

Topping:

1 c. brown sugar, packed
1 c. chopped nuts

1/3 c. all-purpose flour
2-1/2 T. margarine, melted

Blend all ingredients in a small bowl.

*Keep your favorite cookbooks close at hand
tucked inside an old-fashioned market basket.*

Country Sides

Luke's Favorite Potatoes

Mary-Sue Bartlett
Cedar Falls, IA

When I want to make something extra special for my son, Luke, this is the recipe I turn to.

8 to 9 potatoes
2 c. half-and-half
1/2 c. butter

1/2 T. salt
1 c. shredded Cheddar cheese
1/2 c. grated Parmesan cheese

In a large saucepan, cover unpeeled potatoes with water and boil until tender; drain. When completely cool, peel potatoes and shred into a large mixing bowl. In a small saucepan, mix half-and-half, butter and salt; cook until warm. Pour over shredded potatoes and mix well. Transfer to a buttered 2-quart casserole dish. Cover with a layer of Cheddar cheese and a layer of Parmesan cheese. Refrigerate overnight. Bake at 350 degrees for about one hour. Serves 8.

Potatoes are to food what sensible shoes are
to fashion.

– Linda Wells

Creamy Broccoli Stuffing

Carol Shirkey
Canton, OH

A cheesy side dish your family will love.

10-oz. pkg. chopped broccoli, frozen
1-1/2 T. butter, melted
2-1/2 T. all-purpose flour

3/4 c. milk
6-oz. pkg. herbed stuffing mix
1/4 lb. pasteurized process cheese, sliced

Cook broccoli according to package directions; drain. Melt butter in another saucepan. Add flour and milk, cook until thickened. Prepare stuffing mix according to directions on package. Lightly oil a 2-quart casserole dish. Layer 1/2 of broccoli and 1/2 of cheese slices in bottom of dish. Spread a layer of butter mixture over cheese, and then add a layer of stuffing. Repeat layers as above, ending with stuffing. Bake, uncovered, at 350 degrees for 30 minutes. Serves 6 to 8.

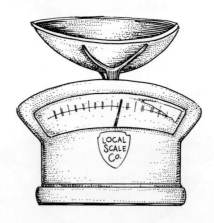

The best way to cheer yourself up is to try
to cheer someone else up.

–Mark Twain

Scalloped Potatoes

*Mary Hanson
Centerville, WA*

*A special recipe to me because I received it from my mother-in-law
shortly after I was married.*

1/2 c. onion, chopped
1/2 c. butter
4 lbs. potatoes, peeled
salt and pepper to taste
2 c. sour cream
2 10-3/4 oz. cans cream of
  mushroom soup

2 10-3/4 oz. cans cream of
  celery soup
1-1/2 c. shredded Cheddar
  cheese
1 c. corn flake cereal, crushed

Sauté onions in butter and set aside. Cover potatoes with water; boil
until tender. Drain; cut up into bite-size chunks. Mix all ingredients
except cereal with onion. Spread mixture into a 3-quart casserole dish
and bake at 350 degrees for one hour. Sprinkle crushed
cereal over casserole during the last 15 minutes. Makes
8 to 10 servings.

An old seed display crate looks wonderful
white-washed and filled with herbs, rolled up
homespun towels, or dried flowers tucked inside.

Special Supper Stuffing

Carol Bull
Delaware, OH

Some of my fondest memories have been made antiquing with two dear friends through our local Amish community. We spend the day looking for treasures that "need a home" and then have lunch at a wonderful family-style restaurant that features traditional Amish foods. This "one-dish meal" reminds me of good friends and good times every time I serve it. It's scrumptious served with homemade bread and cabbage slaw.

2 1-lb. loaves white bread	1 T. dried sage
2 lbs. chicken breasts, poached	1 t. dried thyme
1/2 c. fresh parsley, minced	1 t. pepper
1 c. onion, chopped	5 eggs, beaten
3/4 c. celery, chopped	12-oz. can evaporated milk
1 c. carrot, peeled and shredded	2-1/2 c. chicken broth
1-1/4 c. potatoes, peeled, boiled & finely chopped	

Cube bread and toast on baking sheets at 350 degrees for 15 minutes. Transfer to a very large mixing bowl. Shred and chop chicken breasts and add to bread cubes. Mix in vegetables and seasonings; toss. In a medium bowl, beat eggs, milk and broth. Pour over the bread cube mixture and stir gently. Mixture will be very moist. Allow to stand for one hour. Transfer stuffing to an oiled 3-quart glass casserole dish. Bake at 350 degrees for 2 hours, or until center puffs up and is golden brown. Serves 10 to 16.

To be capable of steady friendship or lasting love, are the two greatest proofs, not only of goodness of heart, but strength of mind.

–William Hazlitt

Macaroni Corn Casserole

Judy Kelly
St Charles, MO

I've made this recipe so many times at my children's request,
that it has already become a tradition!

1 c. elbow macaroni, uncooked	1/2 c. margarine
16-oz. can whole kernel corn, undrained	1 c. pasteurized process cheese, diced
17-oz. can cream-style corn	

Mix the macaroni, corn and cream-style corn in a 2-quart casserole dish. Microwave margarine and cheese in a microwave-safe dish until melted. Add to corn mixture; mix well. Bake at 350 degrees for 45 minutes. Serves 6 to 8.

Happiness isn't something you experience:
it's something you remember.

–Oscar Levant

Company Potatoes

Alice Monaghan
St. Joseph, MO

A homestyle, creamy potato casserole that's perfect with any meal!

12 medium potatoes, sliced
1/2 c. milk
1/2 lb. American cheese,
  chopped
1/2 c. shortening
1 green pepper, diced

1 onion, diced
4-oz. jar pimentos, diced
  and drained
1 T. parsley flakes
salt and pepper to taste

Cover unpeeled potatoes with water and boil until tender. Drain and slice. In a medium saucepan, combine milk, cheese and shortening. Cook and stir until melted and smooth. Combine the potatoes, green pepper, onion and pimentos in a large bowl. Add parsley flakes, salt and pepper. Add cheese sauce to this mixture and gently mix together. Transfer to a 3-quart casserole dish. Cover with aluminum foil and bake at 400 degrees for 40 to 50 minutes. Serves 8 to 10.

There was a place in childhood, that I remember well,
and there a voice of sweetest tone, bright airy tales did tell,
and gentle words, and fond embrace, were given with joy to me,
when I was in that happy place upon my mother's knee.

–Samuel Lover

Country Sides

Fruited Yams

Cindy Neel
Gooseberry Patch

This recipe is a good side dish any time of year, but it's especially comforting on blustery, autumn days!

2 yams	1 T. brown sugar, packed
1 c. pineapple, chopped	1 t. lemon zest
1 banana, sliced	1 t. cinnamon
3/4 c. apple, cored and chopped	1/2 t. ginger
1/4 c. raisins	1/4 t. nutmeg
1/3 c. apple juice	

Spray a 13"x9" baking pan with non-stick vegetable spray. Peel and cut yams into 1/4-inch slices. Layer half of the yams in dish. Mix pineapple, banana, apple and raisins. Spread half of the fruit mixture over yams. Repeat with remaining yams and fruit mixture. Mix remaining ingredients. Pour evenly over yams and fruit mixture. Cover and bake at 350 degrees for 50 to 60 minutes or until yams are tender. Serves 6.

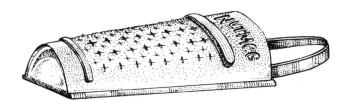

Set little terra cotta pots filled with fresh-growing herbs in a candlebox!

Overnight Potato Casserole

Jennifer Habush
Sherman Oaks, CA

*I've make this dish every Thanksgiving and Christmas since 1977.
I have never had the reputation of being a good cook, so my kind-
hearted mother taught me how to make this delicious and easy recipe.*

16-oz. container sour cream
10-3/4 oz. can cream of
   chicken soup
1-1/2 c. shredded Cheddar
   cheese

1/3 c. yellow onion, minced
1/2 c. plus 1 T. butter, divided
32-oz. pkg. frozen diced
   hashbrowns
1 c. soft bread crumbs

In a large saucepan, combine sour cream, soup, cheese, onion and
1/2 cup butter; stir well. Heat through over medium heat. Stir in
hashbrowns; heat through and spoon into a buttered 13"x9" glass
baking pan. Melt remaining butter and toss with bread crumbs;
sprinkle on top. Cover and refrigerate overnight. Uncover; bake at
350 degrees for one hour, or until bubbly and golden. Serves 6 to 8.

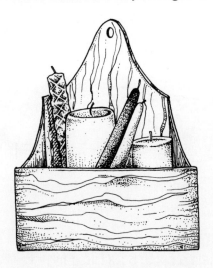

Let the sky rain potatoes!

–Shakespeare

Pickle Relish

Martha Riesterer
Castalia, OH

This dish was handed down to me from my Grandma. I remember making it was so much fun! We would set up the grinder outside on the picnic table and spend hours grinding the ingredients. Over the years, this relish has become a cherished gift to family and friends.

8 qts. pickling cucumbers
1/4 c. salt
6 green peppers
6 red peppers
12 onions
2 bunches celery

3 lbs. sugar
1 qt. vinegar
2 oz. mustard seed
8 canning jars with lids,
    sterilized

Grind pickles and salt together; let stand overnight. Combine peppers, onions and celery; grind well and let stand overnight. In a large bowl, combine sugar, vinegar and mustard seed. Pour over well-drained pickles; blend with remaining ingredients. Transfer to a very large kettle. Heat through and immediately spoon into sterilized jars, leaving 1/4-inch headspace. Add lids and rings. Process 10 minutes in a boiling-water bath. Set jars on towels to cool. Makes 8 pints.

Jars nestled in an old tin tray, are perfect for holding dried herbs from your garden!

Vegetable Herb Trio

Dorothy Jackson
Weddington, NC

Every summer my family can hardly wait for the fresh vegetables to be harvested from the garden so we can prepare this recipe!

1/2 lb. green beans, cut into
   1-1/2 inch pieces
1/2 c. onion, chopped
2 T. fresh parsley, chopped
3/4 t. fresh thyme
3/4 t. fresh sage

1 t. salt
1/8 t. pepper
3/4 c. water, divided
2 c. yellow squash, sliced
3 tomatoes, cut into wedges
2 T. butter

Combine beans, onion, herbs, salt, pepper and 1/2 cup of water in a large skillet. Bring to a boil. Cover skillet; reduce heat and simmer for 10 minutes. Add squash and remaining water to skillet. Bring to a boil. Cover and reduce heat and simmer for another 10 minutes. Drain well. Add tomatoes and butter. Cook, stirring often, until butter melts. Serves 6.

Paint a folk art flag on the lid of your picnic basket!

Country Sides

Escalloped Corn

Carol Shirkey
Canton, OH

An old-fashioned corn dish that's so easy to make.

1/2 c. margarine
2 eggs
8-oz. container sour cream
8-oz. can cream-style corn

8-oz. can whole kernel corn,
   undrained
8-oz. pkg. corn muffin mix

Melt margarine in a pan and pour into a bowl. Beat the eggs and add to margarine. Beat in sour cream, both cans of corn and muffin mix. Mix thoroughly. Spoon batter into a greased 9"x9" baking pan. Bake for one hour at 350 degrees. Serves 9.

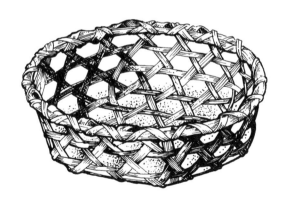

Happiness makes up in height for what it
lacks in length.

–Robert Frost

Copper Pennies

Cheryl Bierley
Miamisburg, OH

An old-fashioned favorite.

2 lbs. carrots, peeled and sliced
1 c. tomato sauce
1 green pepper, diced
3/4 c. onion, diced
1 c. sugar

1/2 c. vinegar
1/4 c. margarine, melted
1/2 t. dry mustard
1/2 t. Worcestershire sauce
salt and pepper to taste

Cook carrots in water until tender; drain well and set aside. In same saucepan, combine remaining ingredients and cook 5 minutes over medium heat. Pour over carrots. Refrigerate at least 2 days to marinate. This dish can be served hot or cold, as a vegetable or relish. Seves 8.

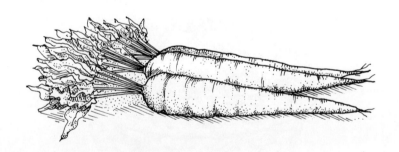

Some people may still have their first dollar, but
the man who is really wealthy is the fellow who
still has his first friend.

– Anonymous

Brown Sugar Beans

Lisa Sabula
Ostrander, OH

An old-fashioned favorite our family loves.

1/4 c. onion, chopped	1/4 c. brown sugar
4 slices bacon, cut in pieces	1 T. Worcestershire sauce
1/2 c. catsup	15-oz. can green beans, drained

Brown onion and bacon in a skillet. Add catsup, brown sugar and Worcestershire sauce. Simmer 2 minutes. Place green beans in a one-quart casserole dish. Pour sauce over beans. Do not stir. Bake at 350 degrees for 20 minutes. Serves 6.

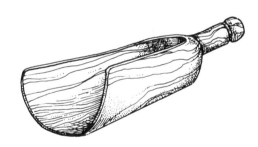

Paint and sand the edges of small mismatched drawers. Stack and fill with potpourri, rosehips, star anise or cinnamon sticks.

Grandma Leland's Red Cabbage

Suzan Detwiler
Easton, PA

Our family especially likes this dish...
it brings back some wonderful memories.

1 head red cabbage, shredded
3 T. shortening
1 onion, sliced
1/2 t. whole cloves

1 c. white vinegar
3 c. water
sugar to taste

Sauté cabbage in shortening. Add remaining ingredients except water and sugar; bring to a boil. Cover and let simmer for about one hour. When cooled, add sugar to taste. Serves 8 to 10.

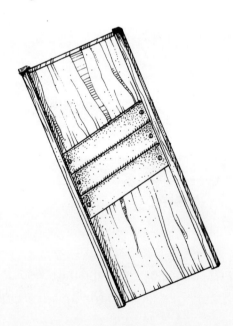

Use a shadowbox to display Grandma's old-fashioned kitchen utensils and her favorite recipe cards.

Pickled Mushrooms

Linda Spain
Ashley, OH

We could always count on Grandma Spain to bring her pickled mushrooms to any family get-together...and they never lasted long! Even though she is no longer with us, we still think of her whenever someone makes this recipe.

1/3 c. red wine vinegar
1/3 c. oil
1/2 c. onion, thinly sliced and
   separated into rings
1 t. salt

2 t. dried parsley
1 t. mustard
1 T. brown sugar, packed
3 4-oz. jars button mushrooms,
   drained

In a small saucepan, combine all ingredients except mushrooms. When mixture comes to a boil, add mushrooms and simmer for 5 minutes. Pour into a bowl; cover and chill for several hours or overnight, stirring occasionally. Drain before serving. Makes 8 to 10 servings.

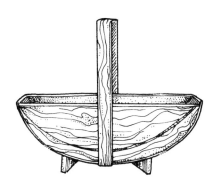

A happy family is but an earlier heaven.

– John Bowring

Birch Bayh Green Beans

Margaretta Wilson
Marshall, IL

This recipe is a Wilson family favorite! My mother-in-law copied the recipe out of a 1964 Democratic Party Cookbook, changing it slightly to suit the tastes of her family. The recipe was named after Birch Bayh, a Senator in Indiana at the time. It was originally submitted to the Democratic cookbook by his wife, who said, "My husband prefers this to ice cream!" My mother-in-law has since passed away, but her daughters-in-law and granddaughters have carried on this traditional dish.

2 14-1/4 oz. cans French-style green beans, drained
10-3/4 oz. can cream of mushroom or cream of celery soup, divided

8 slices pasteurized process cheese, divided
2.8-oz. can French fried onion rings, divided

Pour one can of beans into a 2-quart casserole dish. On top of beans, layer 1/2 can of soup, 4 slices of cheese and 1/2 can of onion rings. Top onion rings with remaining beans, soup and cheese. Bake at 350 degrees for 35 to 45 minutes. Top with remaining onion rings for last 5 minutes of baking. Serves 6 to 8.

The greatest essentials of happiness are
something to do, someone to love,
and something to hope for.

– Joseph Addison

Country Sides

Marinated Vegetables

Jennifer Woodruff
Van Buren, AR

A favorite at our house! It's requested at every family gathering!

14-1/4 oz. can green peas,
   drained
14-1/4 oz. can French-style
   green beans, drained

14-1/4 oz. can corn, drained
1 red pepper, chopped
1/2 c. red onion, chopped

Combine peas, beans and corn in a large bowl. Add chopped pepper and onion; mix well. Toss with dressing; pour over vegetables. Chill overnight for best results. Should be chilled for at least 4 hours. Serves 8.

Dressing:

1 c. sugar
1 c. water
2/3 c. oil

2/3 c. white vinegar
1 t. salt (optional)

Bring ingredients to a boil.

Happiness is like a potato salad...when shared with others,
it's a picnic!

– Anonymous

Butternut Squash

Dorothy Foor
Jeromesville, OH

The crumb topping adds a special crunch!

1-1/2 lbs. butternut squash,
   peeled and cut into cubes
2 T. all-purpose flour
2 T. lemon juice

1 t. cinnamon
1/4 t. salt
1/3 c. dry bread crumbs
2 T. chicken broth

Spray an 8"x8" baking pan with non-stick vegetable spray. Mix all ingredients except bread crumbs and broth. Spread in pan. Bake, uncovered, at 350 degrees for 50 minutes or until squash is tender. Mix bread crumbs and broth. Spread evenly over squash. Set oven control to broil. Broil squash about 4 inches from heat for 3 minutes, or until bread crumbs are brown. Serves 6.

Display your antique pull-toys on a round wooden plant stand.

Country Sides

Garlic Smashed Potatoes

Vickie
Gooseberry Patch

A favorite in our house...sprinkle some chives on top for extra flavor!

5 lbs. redskin potatoes, peeled
    and cubed
1 head garlic
1 T. oil
1/2 c. butter

8-oz. pkg. cream cheese,
    softened
1 c. sour cream
salt to taste

Place potatoes in a Dutch oven; cover with water and bring to a boil. Continue to cook until potatoes are tender. Drain and set aside. Cut garlic horizontally and place in a small baking pan. Drizzle with oil and bake at 350 degrees for 30 minutes or until tender. Using a fork, remove skin and mash garlic. Mash potatoes. Add garlic and remaining ingredients; blend well. Spoon potatoes into a 13"x9" baking pan. Cover and refrigerate overnight. When ready to serve, heat oven to 350 degrees and bake for 50 to 60 minutes. Serves 10.

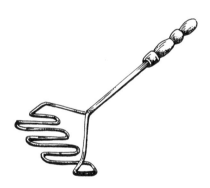

Pray for peace and grace and spiritual food; For wisdom and guidance, for all these are good, But don't forget the potatoes!

–John Tyler Pettee

Zesty Broccoli

Barbara Arnold
Toledo, OH

A touch of horseradish makes this creamy broccoli dish even better!

2 10-oz. pkgs. chopped frozen
   broccoli
10-3/4 oz. can cream of
   mushroom soup
1-1/2 c. shredded Cheddar
   cheese

1 egg, beaten
1/4 c. milk
1/4 c. mayonnaise
1 T. grated horseradish
2 T. butter, melted
1/4 c. cracker crumbs, crushed

Cook broccoli according to package instructions; drain. Combine soup, cheese, egg, milk and mayonnaise. Add horseradish. Stir into broccoli. Spoon into a greased 2-quart casserole dish. Combine butter and crumbs; sprinkle on top. Bake at 350 degrees for 45 minutes.
Serves 6 to 8

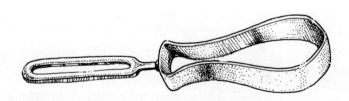

Tuck a votive inside a collection of aged tin or spatterware cups; surround it with rosehips.

Mom's Perky Pickles

Leekay Bennett
Delaware, OH

This recipe is nearly 70 years old. As a child, Mom and I would make these together about every other month. She would cut the pickles, I'd add the sugar and pour the juice back into the jar, then Mom would shake the jar...it gave us quiet time together. The name came about when I bit into my first pickle, puckered up, and announced to my grandmother and mom, "These sure are perky pickles!"

2 qts. whole Kosher dill pickles   2 c. sugar, divided

Pour off the juice from the dill pickles and save. Cut pickles 1/2 to 1-1/2 inches thick. Fill jar with a layer of cut pickles, topped with 1/3 cup sugar. Continue layering until jar is firmly packed. Pour the reserved pickle juice back into the jar and seal tightly; shake to distribute sugar. Refrigerate pickles for 4 to 7 days. Shake the jar once a day to make sure the sugar fully dissolves. Makes 2 quarts.

You've got to get up every morning with a smile on your face, and show the world all the love in your heart.

−Carole King

Glorified Rice

Donna Cozzens
Laramie, WY

This is a special recipe we always enjoyed with our meal. I can still picture my grandmother arriving for a visit. As soon as her car pulled in to the yard, we would rush out to help her carry the bundles of goodies into our house. Our favorite dishes still warm from her oven; the food was always in the original cooking pots, so as not to lose any flavor. Each dish was wrapped up in a white kitchen dish towel with a tidy knot and handle at the top for carrying. When all of the towels were unfolded we would eagerly gather for dinner. Even though Grandma had transported dinner from her kitchen over the miles to our home, we loved the idea she provided for us...the comforting feeling that we were visiting Grandma's home.

1 c. long-cooking rice, uncooked
16-oz. can crushed pineapple in
   heavy syrup
3-oz. pkg. vanilla pudding mix

1-3/4 c. milk
2 T. sugar
1 c. whipped cream
Garnish: maraschino cherries

Boil one cup of rice according to package directions. Drain and cool. Drain pineapple and add it to the rice. Combine pudding and milk. Mixture should be thick, not thin. Add sugar and chill. Mix pudding, rice and pineapple together. Spread in a 9"x9" glass baking pan. Spread the top with whipped cream and decorate to your liking with maraschino cherries. Serves 6 to 8.

The world is your cow,
but you must milk it.

–Vermont saying

Corn & Tomatoes

LaRayne Cummons
Lakeview, OH

Just-picked vegetables from your garden or the farmers' market make this side dish perfect for a warm weather family picnic!

6 tomatoes	1/2 t. pepper
2 c. fresh corn	1 t. fresh chives, chopped
1/2 t. salt	1/4 t. dried basil

In a saucepan, pour boiling water over tomatoes. Cool slightly. Slip off tomato skins and chop tomatoes. Combine corn and tomatoes in a saucepan. Add salt, pepper, chives and basil. Simmer over low heat for 20 minutes, or until vegetables are tender. Serves 6.

An aged wooden checkerboard hung on the wall is perfect for displaying dried flowers or herbs on old tin hooks.

Whipped Sweet Potatoes

Betty Stout
Worthington, OH

Good with lots of melting butter on top!

3 lbs. sweet potatoes, peeled and
    cut into 1-inch pieces
4 carrots, peeled and cut into
    1-inch pieces
2 chicken bouillon cubes

6 T. unsalted butter
1/4 c. light brown sugar, packed
2 T. fresh orange juice
1 T. ground nutmeg
salt, to taste

Combine sweet potatoes, carrots and bouillon cubes in a large heavy pot and cover with cold water. Bring to a boil. Reduce heat and simmer until vegetables are very tender, 15 to 20 minutes. Drain, reserving 6 tablespoons of the cooking liquid; place in a bowl. With an electric mixer, whip vegetables with reserved cooking liquid and remaining ingredients. Serve immediately or bake, covered, at 350 degrees for 15 to 20 minutes. Serves 6 to 8.

*Oh, potatoes, they grow small, for they plant them in the fall
and they eat 'em skins and all, in Kansas.*

– Kansas song

Grandma's Baked Goods

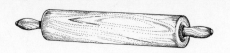

While we were growing up, the hot summer days were offset by the fun of enjoying homemade ice cream! Mom would pour a mixture of fresh cream, sugar and milk into our wooden ice cream maker, pack it with ice and salt, secure the lid, and the cranking began!

At first it was easy to crank the handle, even the littlest one could easily do it; however, the job became more difficult as the ice cream hardened. Dad would always have to finish the last few turns, just for good measure! When he removed the lid, there was a crowd of children wanting to lick the dasher after it was removed from the bucket! There was nothing like fresh, homemade ice cream on a hot summer day.

After our homemade treat, we would take turns in the simple tree swing, trying to touch the sky with our toes! Mom would settle in a hammock, fanning herself with a wide-brimmed straw hat.

Honey Bun Cake

Carol Lankford
Danville, VA

Our family loves this cake!

18-1/2 oz. yellow cake mix	1 c. brown sugar, packed
4 eggs, beaten	2 t. cinnamon
3/4 c. oil	1/2 c. chopped pecans
1 c. buttermilk	

Combine cake mix, eggs, oil and buttermilk; beat well. Pour into a greased 13"x9" baking pan. Combine brown sugar, cinnamon and pecans. Swirl into batter. Bake at 300 degrees for 40 to 60 minutes. Check after 40 minutes with a toothpick. Makes 12 to 15 servings.

Glaze:

1 c. powdered sugar	1 t. vanilla extract
2 T. milk	

Mix all ingredients together and pour over warm cake.

Old twigs tied together can make a primitive frame for your sampler.

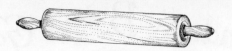

Sour Cream Apple Squares

Pat Habiger
Spearville, KS

Just like apple pie!

2 c. all-purpose flour
2 c. brown sugar, packed
1/2 c. margarine, softened
1/2 c. chopped nuts
2 t. cinnamon
1 t. baking soda
1/2 t. salt

1 c. sour cream
1 t. vanilla extract
1 egg, beaten
2 c. apples, cored, peeled
   and chopped
Garnish: whipped cream

In a mixing bowl, combine flour, brown sugar and margarine; beat with an electric mixer on low speed until crumbly. Stir in nuts. Press about 2-3/4 cups of crumb mixture into the bottom of an ungreased 13"x9" baking pan. To the remaining crumb mixture, add cinnamon, baking soda, salt, sour cream, vanilla and egg. Beat until thoroughly combined. Stir in apples. Spoon evenly over bottom layer. Bake at 350 degrees for 35 to 40 minutes. Cool on wire rack. Cut into squares. Garnish with whipped cream. Makes 12 to 15 servings.

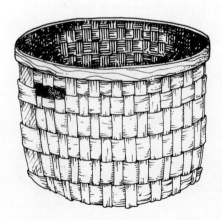

An apple pie without some cheese
is like a kiss without a squeeze.

– English proverb

Grandma's Baked Goods

Mystery Pecan Pie

Valeri McCown
Auberry, CA

The mystery is how the layers reverse positions while baking!
Everyone who tastes this pie will want the recipe!

8–oz. pkg. cream cheese,
   softened
1/3 c. plus 1/4 c. sugar, divided
1/4 t. salt
2 t. vanilla extract, divided
4 eggs, divided

9-inch pie crust, unbaked
1-1/4 c. chopped pecans
1 c. light corn syrup
Garnish: whipped cream

Beat together cream cheese, 1/3 cup sugar, salt, one teaspoon vanilla and one egg. Pour into pie crust. Sprinkle pecans over cream cheese layer. Beat together remaining eggs, sugar and vanilla; beat in corn syrup. Pour this mixture over pecan layer. Bake at 375 degrees for 35 to 40 minutes, until filling is firm. Refrigerate before serving. Top with whipped cream. Serves 6 to 8.

Old-fashioned canning jars are great for storing cookie cutters.

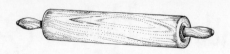

Oatmeal Cake

Teresa Cates
Odessa, TX

I remember this recipe as a dessert that my mother prepared on many occasions. Everyone would always compliment her, and now that I'm continuing the tradition, I'm the one getting the compliments... but I owe it all to her.

1 c. rolled oats, uncooked
1-1/2 c. boiling water
1/2 c. butter
1 c. sugar
1 c. brown sugar, packed

2 eggs, beaten
1/8 t. salt
1-1/2 c. all-purpose flour
1 t. baking soda
1 t. cinnamon

Mix oats and boiling water. Let stand for 20 minutes. Blend butter and sugars together. Add eggs and salt; combine with oats. Stir in flour, baking soda and cinnamon. Pour into a greased and floured 13"x9" baking pan. Bake at 325 degrees for 35 minutes. Spoon Icing over warm cake. Place under broiler until bubbly. Makes 12 to 15 servings.

Icing:

3/4 c. butter
1 c. brown sugar, packed
1/2 c. half-and-half

1 c. chopped pecans
2 c. flaked coconut

Mix all ingredients together.

Hold a true friend with both
thy hands.

– Nigerian Proverb

Fudgy-Topped Brownies

Carole Foltman
Williams Bay, WI

These truly satisfy a chocolate craving!

1/2 c. butter
1 c. sugar
4 eggs, beaten
1 c. all-purpose flour

16-oz. can chocolate syrup
1 t. vanilla extract
1 c. chopped nuts

Blend together butter and sugar. Add eggs, flour, chocolate syrup, vanilla and nuts. Bake in a 13"x9" baking pan at 350 degrees for 40 minutes; or a 15"x10" jelly-roll pan for 20 minutes. Sppread frosting over warm brownies. Makes 15 servings.

Frosting:

1-1/3 c. sugar
6 T. butter

6 T. milk
6-oz. pkg. chocolate chips

Combine sugar, butter and milk in a saucepan; stir until sugar is completely dissolved. Bring to a boil for one minute. Remove from heat and add chocolate chips. Mix quickly until chips melt.

A copper boiler filled with kindling gives a feeling of
Grandma's kitchen when set next to your stove.

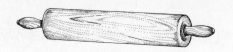

Praline-Apple Crisp

Cheryl Bierley
Miamisburg, OH

Serve warm with a little milk poured over top.

1 T. water
1 t. almond extract
6 c. tart apples, cored and sliced
2 T. margarine
2 T. all-purpose flour

2 T. brown sugar, packed
1/2 t. cinnamon, ground
1/2 c. zwieback crackers,
   crushed
2 T. chopped pecans

Spray a 1-1/2 quart casserole dish with non-stick vegetable spray. Mix water and almond extract; toss with apples in casserole. Cut margarine into flour, brown sugar and cinnamon with a pastry blender in a small bowl until mixture is crumbly. Stir in crackers and pecans. Sprinkle over apples. Bake, uncovered, at 375 degrees for about 30 minutes, or until top is golden brown and apples are tender. Serve warm. Serves 6.

Old quilt rag balls look wonderful spilling from a gathering basket! Display them on your step-back cupboard or on a dry sink.

Blackberry Cobbler

Judy Cheatham
Brentwood, TN

This cobbler is so delicious...the crust rises to the surface!
We love it served with a big scoop of vanilla ice cream!

1/2 c. butter	1/2 t. nutmeg
1 c. all-purpose flour	1/2 c. half-and-half
2 c. sugar, divided	1 t. vanilla extract
1 t. baking powder	2 c. blackberries

Preheat oven to 350 degrees. Melt butter in a 9"x9" baking pan in the oven. In a medium bowl, whisk together flour, one cup sugar, baking powder and nutmeg. Combine half-and-half and vanilla in a measuring cup, then add to the flour mixture blending until crumbly. Press dough into baking pan on top of the butter; some butter will spill over onto the dough. In a medium saucepan, stir together berries with remaining sugar. Warm over low heat and pour over dough. Bake at 350 degrees for 50 to 55 minutes or until the crust is golden brown. Serves 6 to 8.

A milkman's old-fashioned bottle carrier makes a wonderful picnic basket! Fill it with lunch, canning jars full of icy lemonade and tie a bandanna napkin on the handle.

Strawberry Shortcake

Terri Harkins
Philadelphia, PA

When my grandmother wrote this recipe down, everything was a pinch of this and a dash of that. I remember it because my grandmother was the best cook! I will always remember the smell of her kitchen, and this recipe brings her closer to me.

2 eggs
1 c. sugar
1 t. vanilla extract
1 c. all-purpose flour
1 t. baking powder

1/2 c. milk
3 T. butter
1 pt. heavy cream, whipped
2 c. strawberries, sliced
powdered sugar to taste

Beat eggs and sugar together. Continue beating and add vanilla. Combine flour and baking powder; add to the egg and sugar mixture. Heat milk and butter, then add to mixture. Grease and flour a 9"x9" pan, pour in mixture. Bake at 350 degrees for 20 minutes. This makes one layer. For 2 layers repeat recipe. Cool cake. Spread cake with whipped cream, sliced strawberries, and sprinkle with powdered sugar when serving. Makes 8 servings.

Build a shelf out of barn siding or discarded boards, then paint, stain and sand the edges to make it look old. Attach hooks and hang a kitchen collection of enamel cups, a potato masher, sifter or pastry blender.

German Chocolate Pie

Pauline Raens
Abilene, TX

A quick and easy recipe for family gatherings.

2 1-oz. sqs. German sweet
   baking chocolate
1 c. butter
3 eggs, beaten
2 T. all-purpose flour
1 c. sugar

1 t. vanilla extract
1 c. chopped pecans
1/2 c. coconut
Garnish: whipped cream, shaved
   chocolate and pecans

Melt chocolate and butter in a saucepan over low heat and let cool. With an electric mixer, beat eggs, flour, sugar and vanilla together at high speed for 3 minutes. Pour chocolate mixture over eggs and beat 3 more minutes. Add pecans and coconut. Pour into a well-buttered 9" pie plate. Bake at 350 degrees for 28 minutes. Cool just before serving. Top with whipped cream and garnish with shaved chocolate and pecans. Serves 8.

I always have a chair for you in the
smallest parlor in the world,
to wit, my heart.

–Emily Dickinson

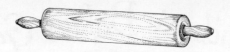

Warm Turtle Cake

Laurie Benham
Playas, New Mexico

A cake that reminds me of the boxes of chocolate-covered turtles that my dad used to bring home for us when we were little!

1 box Swiss chocolate cake mix
1/3 c. plus 1/2 c. evaporated
   milk, divided
3/4 c. butter, melted

14-oz. pkg. caramels,
   unwrapped
1 c. pecan pieces
3/4 c. semi-sweet chocolate chips

Beat together cake mix, 1/3 cup evaporated milk and melted butter with an electric mixer on medium speed for 2 minutes. Pour half of batter into a greased 11"x7" baking pan. Bake at 350 degrees for 6 minutes. In a double boiler or microwave, melt remaining evaporated milk and caramels. Drizzle over cake. Sprinkle pecan pieces and chocolate chips over caramels. Use a wet knife to spread the remaining cake batter over the pecan pieces and chocolate chips. Bake at 350 degrees for 18 minutes. Makes 6 to 8 servings.

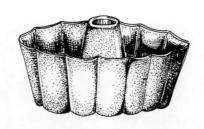

Create your own seasoning mixes from herbs
in your garden! For gift-giving, tuck them inside
plastic-lined homespun bags tied with raffia.

Grandma's Baked Goods

Grandma Eddy's Apple Crumble

Mary Warren
Auburn, MI

An old family favorite that brings back memories of our visits to my husband's mother's and grandmother's homes. There was always a dish of apple, cherry, blueberry or blackberry crumble around whenever we stopped to visit. When my children were small, I started making this family recipe and now my daughter and son help carry on the family tradition.

3/4 c. margarine, softened
3/4 c. all-purpose flour
3/4 c. brown sugar, packed
3/4 c. quick-cooking oats,
   uncooked

1/8 t. salt
4 to 6 apples, peeled, cored
   and sliced
cinnamon to taste
1/4 c. sugar

Mix margarine, flour, brown sugar, oats and salt until crumbly; set aside. Place apples in a 13"x9" baking pan; sprinkle with cinnamon and sugar. Sprinkle brown sugar topping over all and bake at 375 degrees for 30 minutes, or until topping is lightly browned and crunchy. Makes 12 servings.

If you have built castles in the air, your work need not be lost; that is where they should be. Now put foundations under them.

– Henry David Thoreau

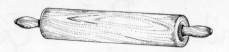

Peanut Butter Pie

Deb Robb
Lucas, IA

Chocolate and peanut butter...perfect together!

8-oz. pkg. cream cheese
1 c. sugar
1 c. chunky peanut butter
1 t. vanilla extract
2 T. butter, melted

12-oz. container frozen whipped
    topping, thawed and divided
2 T. chocolate ice cream topping,
    warmed

Soften cream cheese to room temperature. Combine with sugar, peanut butter and vanilla. Mix well. Add melted butter. Fold in whipped topping, reserving one cup. Pour into prepared crust. Drizzle pie with chocolate ice cream topping. Serve with remaining whipped topping. Serves 6 to 8.

Chocolate Cookie Crust:

1-1/2 c. chocolate sandwich
    cookies, finely crushed

6 T. butter, melted

Mix cookies with butter and firmly press into a 9" pie plate. Chill until ready to use.

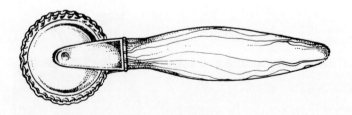

A friend is a present which you give yourself.

– Robert Louis Stevenson

Grandma's Baked Goods

Molasses Sugar Cookies

Mary Sewell
Milford, CT

When I bake these cookies, the smell reminds me of when my children were little. When they came home from school and realized I'd made them, they would jump for joy!

3/4 c. shortening	2 t. baking soda
1 c. sugar	1/2 t. ground cloves
1/4 c. molasses	1/2 t. ground ginger
1 egg, beaten	1 t. cinnamon
2 c. all-purpose flour	1/2 t. salt

Melt shortening and cool. Add sugar, molasses and egg. Beat well. In another bowl, sift together flour, baking soda, spices and salt. Combine with shortening mixture. Mix and chill for 4 hours. Form into one-inch balls and roll in sugar. Place on greased baking sheets. Bake at 375 degrees for 8 to 10 minutes. Cool and enjoy. Makes about 4 dozen.

Live decently, fearlessly, joyously and don't forget that in the long run it is not the years in your life but the life in your years that counts!

–Adlai Stevenson

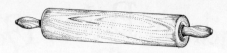

Fresh Peach Pie

Susan Brzozowski
Ellicott City, MD

It's a tradition for my mom and me to make fruit pies when she visits. While making the pies, I have the pleasure of Mom's company as well as her help; then we share this family favorite with my husband and daughter that evening. I freeze a second pie to enjoy the taste and memories when Mom can't be with us.

1 c. sugar
2-1/2 T. cornstarch
1/4 t. salt
1/2 c. water

4 to 5 c. peaches, peeled, pitted
  and sliced
1 T. lemon juice
Optional: 2 to 3 t. milk

Combine sugar, cornstarch and salt in a large saucepan. Add water and peaches. Bring to a boil and boil for one minute, stirring constantly. Cool on a wire rack; add lemon juice. Pour cooled peach mixture into a 9" pie crust. Roll the remaining pie crust dough and fit over top. Seal the edges well and cut vents in top. Bake on lower shelf of oven at 425 degrees for 50 minutes. If desired, brush milk over crust to aid in browning. Makes 6 servings.

Standard Pie Crust:

2 c. all-purpose flour, sifted
1 t. salt

3/4 c. shortening
4 T. cold water

Put flour and salt in mixing bowl and mix. Cut in shortening as follows: For a tender crust, cut in about 2/3 of the shortening with pastry blender or 2 knives until as fine as meal. For a flaky crust, cut in the remaining shortening to the size of large peas. Sprinkle all the water, one tablespoon at a time, over mixture. Mix thoroughly with fork until all particles cling together and form a dough. Using your hands, work crust into a smooth ball. Roll out on a floured board or cloth.

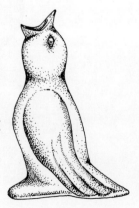

Grandma's Baked Goods

Aunt Esther's Chocolate Chip Cookies
Cindy Caretto
Irvine, CA

Aunt Esther was a wonderful cook. I can't take these cookies anywhere without being asked for the recipe! Butterscotch or chocolate instant pudding may be substituted for the vanilla pudding. Chocolate candies or butterscotch chips may replace the chocolate chips.

1 c. butter, softened
1/4 c. sugar
3/4 c. brown sugar, packed
3-1/2 oz. pkg. instant vanilla
   pudding mix
1 t. baking soda

1 t. vanilla extract
2 eggs, beaten
2-1/2 c. all-purpose flour
2 c. semi-sweet chocolate chips
Optional: 1 c. chopped nuts

Beat together butter, sugar, brown sugar, pudding mix, baking soda and vanilla. Beat in eggs. Add flour and stir together. Stir in chocolate chips and nuts. Drop by heaping teaspoonfuls about 2 inches apart on ungreased baking sheets. Bake for 9-1/2 minutes at 375 degrees. Makes 4 dozen.

If you would be loved, love and be loveable.

– Benjamin Franklin

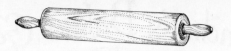

Chocolate Mayonnaise Cake

Debby Sprechman
Pembroke Pines, FL

So rich and moist! It always reminds me of our special family visits.

2 c. all-purpose flour
2 t. baking soda
1-1/4 c. baking cocoa
1/2 t. salt

1 c. mayonnaise
1 c. sugar
1 c. cold coffee
2 t. vanilla extract

Combine flour, baking soda, cocoa and salt; set aside. In a bowl, blend mayonnaise and sugar with an electric mixer on medium speed. Gradually beat in coffee and vanilla. Add flour mixture and beat until well blended; batter will be thick. Spread into a greased and floured 11"x7" baking pan. Bake at 350 degrees for 30 to 35 minutes or until done. Cool and frost. Serves 6 to 8.

Frosting:

2 T. butter
1 c. powdered sugar

1 to 2 t. milk
1 t. vanilla extract

Blend all ingredients together, adjusting milk until the desired consistency is achieved.

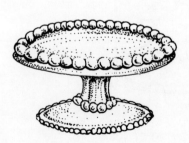

Attach a wooden board to the top
of an old window frame.
Add little wire hooks to
the front edge of the shelf
to hold a collection
of old-fashioned
kitchen utensils.

Grandma's Baked Goods

Old-Fashioned Raspberry Cut-Outs

Rebecca LaDue
Oshkosh, WI

These cookies represent many happy memories of special past occasions. The recipe is over 90 years old, given to my mother by an elderly neighbor who was like a grandmother to me.

1 c. butter, room temperature
1/2 c. sugar
1 c. walnuts, finely chopped

2 c. all-purpose flour
Garnish: additional sugar,
   raspberry jam

Blend butter and sugar. Chop the walnuts in a food processor or blender to nearly a paste consistency. Blend flour and chopped walnuts into butter mixture. Roll out onto a floured surface and cut into your favorite shapes. Bake at 350 degrees on ungreased baking sheets for 10 minutes. Be careful not to overbake; cookies should be soft. When warm, roll in sugar and fill with jam, pressing 2 cookies gently together. Makes 2 to 3 dozen cookies, depending on size of your cookie cutter.

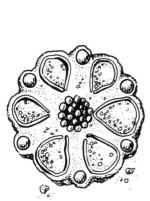

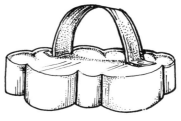

If the world seems cold to you,
kindle fires to warm it.

–Lucy Larcom

Apple Dumplings

Kathy Wheeler
Hillsdale, NY

This recipe was handed down to me from my mother. Many years ago, Mom made three recipe books; one for each of her children. She filled the pages with her favorite recipes and some that were handed down from my grandmother. These recipe books were meant to be given to us at Christmas, but two days before Christmas Mom passed away unexpectedly. These books are a treasure...a part of her that we'll always have. This is my favorite recipe from that book.

2 c. all-purpose flour
4 t. baking powder
1/4 t. salt
2 T. sugar
2 T. shortening

1 c. milk
6 baking apples, peeled, cored
    and chopped
1/2 c. water

Mix flour, baking powder, salt and sugar; blend in shortening with a fork. Add milk gradually and blend with a fork until dough is soft. Set aside. In a heavy saucepan, add apples and enough water to keep apples from sticking while cooking. Cover; bring to a boil and add dumpling dough by spoonfuls over apples. Cover; reduce heat to medium and cook 12 to 15 minutes. Uncover saucepan so dumplings don't become soggy. Serve Vanilla Sauce over dumplings. Serves 6.

Vanilla Sauce:

1-1/2 c. water
1 T. lemon zest
1/2 c. sugar
1-1/2 T. cornstarch

1-1/2 t. vanilla extract
2 T. margarine
1/2 t. cinnamon
1/8 t. nutmeg

Boil water with lemon zest. Mix sugar and cornstarch; add to water, stirring constantly, and cook until thickened. Remove from heat. Add vanilla, margarine, cinnamon and nutmeg.

Grandma Runkle's Sugar Cakes
Julie Bell
New Market, VA

This recipe belonged to my great-grandmother. I remember it well because no one would make these sugar cakes like Grandma Runkle! When I was growing up, I spent Saturday mornings with my great-grandparents and the first thing I would be asked when I arrived was, "Julia, would you like something to eat? I have sugar cakes!" They were the best!

2 c. sugar
1 c. butter
3 eggs, beaten
2 t. baking soda

1 c. buttermilk
1 t. baking powder
4 c. all-purpose flour
1/2 t. salt

Lightly oil a baking sheet and set aside. Mix sugar and butter. Add eggs and beat well. Add baking soda to buttermilk. Sift baking powder with flour and salt. Add flour and milk alternately to sugar mixture. Pour batter onto baking sheet in the size of a silver dollar, and bake at 350 degrees for 10 minutes. Makes 5 to 6 dozen.

Decorate with flea-market finds such as metal basket holders, colorful glasses, or glass drawer pulls...they'll bring back a feeling of comfort from Grandma's house.

Texas Sheet Cake

Jean Shaffer
Washington Court House, OH

Family and friends will look forward to eating this chocolate cake!

2 c. all-purpose flour
2 c. sugar
1/2 t. salt
1/2 c. shortening
1/2 c. margarine
1 c. water

3 T. baking cocoa
2 eggs, beaten
1/2 c. buttermilk
1 t. baking soda
1 t. vanilla extract
Garnish: chopped walnuts

In a large bowl, mix flour, sugar and salt. In a saucepan mix together shortening, margarine, water and cocoa. Bring to a boil; mix with flour mixture. In a small bowl, mix eggs, buttermilk, baking soda and vanilla. Add to cocoa mixture. Combine well; pour batter onto a greased and floured rimmed baking sheet. Bake at 350 degrees for 25 minutes. During last 5 minutes of baking, prepare icing. Ice immediately while cake is hot; sprinkle with walnuts. Serves 15.

Icing:

1/2 c. margarine
3 T. baking cocoa
4 c. powdered sugar

1 t. vanilla extract
4 T. milk

Melt margarine and cocoa. Then add powdered sugar, vanilla and milk. Stir until smooth.

The ornament of a house is the friends who frequent it.

– Ralph Waldo Emerson

Grandma's Baked Goods

Raspberry Nut Pinwheels

Pat Habiger
Spearville, KS

Pat won first prize in a holiday baking contest with this recipe!

2 c. all-purpose flour
1 t. baking powder
1/2 c. margarine, softened
1 c. sugar

1 egg, beaten
1 t. vanilla extract
1/4 c. seedless raspberry jam
1 c. walnuts, finely chopped

Sift together flour and baking powder. Beat together margarine, sugar and egg in a large bowl until fluffy. Stir in vanilla. Gradually add flour mixture, stirring until well combined. Roll out dough between 2 pieces of wax paper to a 12"x10" rectangle. Remove top piece of wax paper. Spread jam evenly over entire surface of dough. Sprinkle with nuts. Firmly roll up dough from the long side, removing wax paper. Refrigerate several hours or overnight. When ready to make cookies, cut roll into generous 1/4-inch slices with a sharp knife. Transfer slices to an ungreased baking sheet, spacing 2 inches apart. Bake at 375 degrees for 9 minutes or until golden around edges. Cool on wire racks. Makes 3 dozen.

Just the knowledge that a good book is awaiting one at the end of a long day makes that day happier.

–Kathleen Norris

Carrot Cake

Karen Moran
Navasota, TX

*I remember my mother baking this for my father's birthday...
it was his favorite cake!*

4 eggs, lightly beaten
1-1/2 c. oil
2-1/2 c. sugar
3 c. all-purpose flour
2 t. baking powder
2 t. baking soda
1 t. salt

2 t. cinnamon
3 c. carrots, peeled and grated
15-1/4 oz. can crushed
   pineapple, drained
1-1/2 to 2 c. chopped nuts
1 t. vanilla extract

In a large mixing bowl, combine eggs, oil and sugar, blending well. Add flour, baking powder, baking soda, salt and cinnamon; stir until smooth. Stir in carrots, pineapple, nuts and vanilla. Pour into 3 greased and floured 9" round cake pans. Bake at 350 degrees for 25 to 30 minutes, or until done. Cool in pans for 10 minutes. Remove from pans and cool completely. Spread Frosting between layers and over cooled cake. Serves 16.

Frosting:

2 8-oz. pkgs. cream cheese,
   softened
1/2 c. margarine
2 16-oz. pkgs. powdered
   sugar, sifted

2 t. vanilla extract
1 c. chopped nuts

Blend together all ingredients.

A friend may well be reckoned the masterpiece of nature.

– Ralph Waldo Emerson

Chocolate Refrigerator Cookies
Judy Kelly
St. Charles, MO

*My mom rarely uses a recipe when she cooks, but she found
this one in a cookbook that I gave her years ago
and has been making them every since.*

1-1/4 c. butter, softened
1-1/2 c. powdered sugar
1 egg, beaten

3 c. cake flour
1/2 c. baking cocoa
1/4 t. salt

Thoroughly mix butter, sugar and egg. Blend in flour, cocoa and salt.
Cover and chill for one hour. Divide dough in half. Shape each half
into a roll 1-1/2 inches in diameter. Wrap and chill at least 8 hours.
Cut rolls into 1/8-inch slices. If dough crumbles while cutting, let
warm slightly. Place one inch apart on ungreased baking sheets.
Bake at 400 degrees for about 8 minutes. Immediately remove from
baking sheets and cool. Frost with Fudge Frosting. Makes 8 dozen.

Fudge Frosting:

1/4 c. shortening
1/3 c. milk
1 c. sugar
2 sqs. unsweetened baking
    chocolate, melted

1/4 t. salt
1 t. vanilla extract

In a saucepan, bring all ingredients
except vanilla to a rolling boil, stirring
occasionally. Boil one minute without stirring. Place pan in a bowl of
ice and water. Beat until frosting is thick and cold. Stir in vanilla.

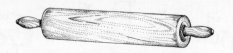

Dutch Apple Cake

Neta Liebscher
El Reno, OK

When our apples are ripe on the tree in the front yard,
it's time to bake a family favorite!

1/2 c. shortening
1/2 c. brown sugar, packed
1 egg
1/4 c. milk
1 c. all-purpose flour
1 t. baking powder
1/2 t. cinnamon

1 c. shredded Cheddar cheese,
   divided
3-1/2 c. apples, peeled, cored
   and chopped
1 t. cinnamon
1/2 c. sugar
1/2 c. chopped nuts

Blend together shortening, brown sugar and egg. Add milk, flour, baking powder and cinnamon. Stir in 1/2 of Cheddar cheese. Pour batter into a greased and floured Bundt® pan. Mix together apples, cinnamon, sugar and nuts. Sprinkle over batter in Bundt® pan. Bake at 325 degrees for 30 minutes. Top with remaining Cheddar cheese while still hot. Let cool; remove from pan and serve. Makes 16 servings.

A house is a home when
it shelters the body and comforts the soul.

–Phillip Moffitt

Grandma's Baked Goods

Sherry's Spicy Cut-Outs

Terri Vanden Bosch
Rock Valley, IA

This recipe was given to me by a dear friend and since then it's become a favorite at our house!

1 c. margarine, softened
1 c. sugar
1/2 c. brown sugar, packed
1 egg
1/4 c. molasses
1 t. salt
1 t. baking soda
1/2 t. baking powder

1 t. cinnamon
1/2 t. ginger
1/2 t. nutmeg
3 c. all-purpose flour
1 c. quick-cooking oats, uncooked
Garnish: favorite frosting

Blend margarine and sugars. Add egg and molasses and beat until fluffy. Sift together remaining ingredients except oats; add gradually to margarine mixture. Stir in oats. Roll out to 1/8-inch thickness on a board sprinkled with powdered sugar. Cut out with cookie cutters. Place on lightly greased baking sheets. Bake at 350 degrees for 7 to 10 minutes. Cool one minute before removing. Frost as desired. Makes 4 to 5 dozen.

Jump into the middle of things,
get your hands dirty, fall flat
on your face, and then
reach for the stars!

– Joan L. Curcio

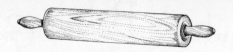

Raisin Crumb Bars

Judy Kelly
St. Charles, MO

This is an old family recipe that makes a tasty dessert.

2 c. raisins
1 c. brown sugar, packed
1 c. butter
1-3/4 c. quick-cooking oats,
    uncooked
1-3/4 c. all-purpose flour
1 t. baking soda

1/2 c. chopped nuts
3 egg yolks
1-1/2 c. sour cream
1 c. sugar
1/4 t. salt
3 T. cornstarch
1 t. cinnamon

Boil raisins in a small amount of water until plump. Drain. Combine brown sugar, butter, oatmeal, flour, baking soda and nuts. Press half of mixture into a 13"x9" baking pan and bake at 350 degrees for 10 minutes. Beat together egg yolks and sour cream in a saucepan. Mix remaining ingredients and add to egg mixture. Cook until thickened. Add raisins. Pour over crust and sprinkle with remaining crumbs. Bake at 350 degrees for 30 minutes. Makes 15 servings.

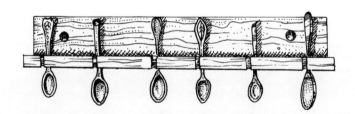

Don't hurry, don't worry.
You're only here for a short visit.
So be sure to stop and smell the flowers.

–Walter Hagen

Grandma's Baked Goods

Sour Cream Pound Cake

Jill Henson
Spruce Pine, NC

When I was young, every Friday and Saturday night we had this wonderful, rich, moist cake! It was a treat I always looked forward to.

1 c. butter
3 c. sugar
6 eggs, beaten
3 c. all-purpose flour, sifted

1/4 t. baking soda
8-oz. container sour cream
1 t. vanilla extract

Beat butter well. Gradually add sugar; beat again. Add eggs, one at a time, beating well after each. Sift together flour and baking soda. Gradually add to butter mixture, alternating with sour cream. Add vanilla. Pour into an oiled tube or Bundt® pan. Bake at 325 degrees for 1-1/2 hours. Test for doneness with a toothpick. Let cake cool in pan for 5 minutes; gently remove. Serves 16.

Oh, cakes and friends we should choose with care.
Not always the fanciest cake that's there is the best to eat!
And the plainest friend is sometimes the finest one in the end.

–Margaret Sangster

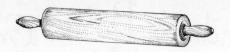

Icebox Brownies

Tami Bowman
Marysville, OH

A chewy brownie that's almost like eating fudge...wonderful!

1/4 c. butter	1/2 c. all-purpose flour
1-1/2 sq. unsweetened baking	1/4 t. baking powder
chocolate	1/4 t. salt
1 egg, beaten	1/4 t. vanilla extract
1 c. brown sugar, packed	1/2 c. chopped walnuts

Melt butter and chocolate in a saucepan over low heat. Using an electric mixer, beat egg, brown sugar and butter-chocolate mixture for 2 minutes. Sift flour, baking powder and salt into mixture. Add vanilla and beat at medium speed for another minute. Stir in walnuts. Pour into greased 8"x8" baking pan and bake at 350 degrees for 15 to 18 minutes (325 degrees for glass pan). Remove from oven and allow to cool. Spread Mint Filling over cooled brownie cake. Chill for an additional 30 minutes in refrigerator. Spread with glaze; cut into squares and store in refrigerator. Makes 12 to 16 servings.

Mint Filling:

1/4 c. butter, softened	2 c. powdered sugar
1/2 t. vanilla extract	2 T. milk
3/4 t. peppermint extract	few drops green food coloring

In a small bowl, beat all ingredients for 2 to 3 minutes until smooth. Let stand in refrigerator until fairly cold and thick, about 30 minutes.

Glaze:

2 sqs. unsweetened baking	1 T. butter
chocolate	

Melt chocolate and butter over low heat.

Grandma's Baked Goods

Peach-Berry Cobbler

Pam Schreiber
Waco, TX

This cobbler is so yummy topped with whipped cream!

18-1/2 oz. pkg. yellow cake mix
1/2 t. cinnamon
1/4 t. nutmeg
1 c. butter, softened
1/2 c. chopped nuts
21-oz. can peach pie filling

16-oz. can whole-berry
   cranberry sauce
Garnish: vanilla ice cream or
   whipped topping

Combine dry cake mix, cinnamon and nutmeg in a bowl. Cut in butter with a pastry blender until crumbly. Stir in nuts and set aside. Combine peach pie filling and cranberry sauce in an ungreased 13"x9" baking pan. Mix well. Sprinkle crumb mixture over the fruit. Bake at 350 degrees for 45 to 50 minutes, or until golden brown. Serve warm with ice cream or whipped topping. Serves 16.

She knew what all smart women knew:
Laughter made you live better and longer.

– Gail Parent

Mom's Apple Crisp

Joan Belitsky
Reading, PA

We had a couple of apple trees at my wonderful childhood home and on the weekends my father would pick the ripe apples and bring them inside. I can remember many a Sunday afternoon, when dusk was beginning to fall, walking through the front door, into our warm home, and smelling Mom's apple crisp. It was a nice way to end the weekend. Now I make it for my own family.

3 to 4 cooking apples, peeled, cored and sliced
1/2 c. butter
3/4 c. brown sugar, packed

3/4 c. quick-cooking oats, uncooked
1/2 c. all-purpose flour
1 t. cinnamon

Arrange apples in an 8"x8" baking pan. Melt butter in a saucepan, stir in remaining ingredients until crumbly. Spread over apples. Bake at 350 degrees for 35 minutes or until apples are soft. Serves 4 to 6.

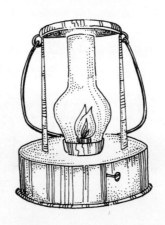

Good friends, good books, and a sleepy conscience: this is the ideal life.

– Mark Twain

Peanut Butter Fudge

Judy Kelly
St. Charles, MO

This is easy to make and so creamy! A great gift for friends.

4-1/2 c. sugar
1-2/3 c. evaporated milk
1/2 c. butter
2 c. crunchy peanut butter

1 c. creamy peanut butter
8-oz. jar marshmallow creme
2 t. vanilla extract

In a saucepan, bring sugar, milk and butter to a boil over medium heat for 8 minutes, stirring constantly. Remove from heat and stir in peanut butter, marshmallow creme and vanilla. Pour into buttered 13"x9" baking pan. Let cool in pan. Cut into squares; wrap individually and box for gifts or store and cut as needed. Makes 3 dozen pieces.

Variation: for chocolate fudge, omit peanut butter. Add a 12-ounce package of semi-sweet chocolate chips and 1/2 cup chopped walnuts, if desired.

Grandma's sewing box looks best left open to view the inside...mismatched buttons, pin cushions, colorful spools of thread and thimbles. All bring back warm memories.

Apple Brown Betty

Tina Stidam
Ashley, OH

Some of my fondest memories are from when I was a little girl spending time with my grandparents. Every Sunday, Granny would fix a feast when the family gathered together. This recipe is one of many I absolutely loved! Grandpa and I would make homemade ice cream to top our dessert. It's a wonderful recipe...I can still smell the aroma in the air.

8 slices white bread, torn
1/2 c. butter, melted
1 t. cinnamon, divided
2-1/2 lbs. Granny Smith apples,
    peeled, cored and sliced

2/3 c. light brown sugar, packed
2 T. lemon juice
1 t. vanilla extract
1/4 t. nutmeg

In a 15"x10" jelly-roll pan, bake bread pieces at 400 degrees until very lightly toasted; about 15 minutes. Stir occasionally. Grease a 2-quart casserole dish; set aside. In a medium bowl, combine butter, 1/2 teaspoon cinnamon and bread; toss gently until evenly moistened. In a large mixing bowl, toss sliced apples, brown sugar, lemon juice, vanilla, nutmeg and remaining cinnamon. Place 1/2 cup bread mixture in casserole dish; top with half the apple mixture. Layer with one cup bread pieces and remaining apple mixture. Toss remaining bread over apple mixture, leaving a one-inch border around the edge. Cover with aluminum foil and bake at 400 degrees for 40 minutes, Uncover and bake 10 minutes longer. Let stand 10 minutes before serving. Serves 8.

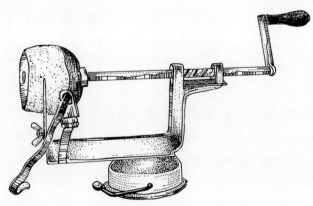

Grandma's Baked Goods

Daisy Brown Sugar Cookies

Kathy Rusert
Mena, AR

My German grandmother kept this cookie dough in the refrigerator so that whenever we came to visit, she always had fresh cookies for us!

2 c. brown sugar, packed
1 c. shortening
2 eggs, beaten
3 c. all-purpose flour

1 t. baking soda
1 t. baking powder
1 t. vanilla extract
1/2 c. chopped pecans

Mix brown sugar, shortening and eggs. Blend well. Add remaining ingredients, mixing well. Roll into 2, 2-inch wide rolls; slice and arrange on baking sheets. Bake at 375 degrees for 8 minutes. Makes 3 dozen

A grandmother is a person with too much wisdom to let that stop her from making a fool of herself over her grandchildren!

– Phil Moss

Index

Breads

Apple-Nut Bread, 34
Aunt Hazel's French Bread, 41
Blueberry Bread, 38
Buttermilk Biscuits, 36
Buttermilk-Chocolate Muffins, 7
Cinnamon Streusel Quick Bread, 42
Cinnamon-Carrot Nut Bread, 37
Coffee Mug Bread, 19
Corn Fritters, 49
Corn Spoon Bread, 43
Country Inn Soda Bread, 45
Country Kitchen Potato Bread, 47
English Muffins, 49
Featherbed Rolls, 31
Garlic Pull-Aparts, 50
Grandma's Special Potato Buns, 32
Grandmother's Rolls, 44
Lemon Clover Rolls, 39
Loving Loaf, 35
Mile-High Biscuits, 46
Muffin Pan Rolls, 40
Poppy Seed Bread, 33
Sour Cream Corn Muffins, 30
Sweet Potato Biscuits, 48
Sweetheart Muffins, 12
The Best Bread in the World, 29

Breakfasts

Amish Sweet Rolls, 13
Apple Fritters, 10
Apple-Stuffed French Toast, 18
Bacon-Cheddar Cups, 23
Blueberry Coffee Cake, 17
Brown Sugar French Toast, 24
Cinnamon Flop, 14
Country Cheese Omelet, 20
Early Riser Home Fries, 26
Farmhouse Sausage Gravy, 21
Flaky Date Scones, 15
Garden-Fresh Denver Omelet, 25
Grammy Irene's Sticky Buns, 8
Orange Breakfast Crescents, 11
Popover Pancake, 9
Rise & Shine Hash Browns, 22
Sugar-Nut Coffee Cake, 16

Condiments

Mom's Perky Pickles, 181
Pickle Relish, 169
Pickled Mushrooms, 175

Cookies

Aunt Esther's Chocolate Chip
    Cookies, 201
Chocolate Refrigerator Cookies, 209
Daisy Brown Sugar Cookies, 219
Fudgy-Topped Brownies, 191
Grandma Runkle's Sugar Cakes, 205
Icebox Brownies, 214
Molasses Sugar Cookies, 199
Old-Fashioned Raspberry Cut-Outs,
    203
Raisin Crumb Bars, 212
Raspberry Nut Pinwheels, 207
Sherry's Spicy Cut-Outs, 211

Desserts

Apple Brown Betty, 218
Apple Dumplings, 204
Blackberry Cobbler, 193
Carrot Cake, 208
Chocolate Mayonnaise Cake, 202
Dutch Apple Cake, 210
Fresh Peach Pie, 200
German Chocolate Pie, 195
Grandma Eddy's Apple Crumble, 197
Honey Bun Cake, 187
Mom's Apple Crisp, 216
Mystery Pecan Pie, 189
Oatmeal Cake, 190
Peach-Berry Cobbler, 215
Peanut Butter Fudge, 217
Peanut Butter Pie, 198
Praline-Apple Crisp, 192
Sour Cream Apple Squares, 188
Sour Cream Pound Cake, 213
Strawberry Shortcake, 194
Texas Sheet Cake, 206
Warm Turtle Cake, 196

Index

Mains

Baked Chicken & Wild Rice, 109
Barbecued Pork Chops, 140
Beef Brisket with Ginger Gravy, 147
Chicken & Biscuits, 118
Chicken & Dumplings, 137
Chicken & Green Bean Bake, 115
Chicken & Stuffing, 150
Chicken Cacciatora, 143
Chicken King Casserole, 124
Chicken Tetrazzini, 106
Colonial Dinner, 129
Country Pork Chops, 127
Country Roast, 136
Deep-Dish Vegetable Pie, 146
Double-Crust Chicken Pot Pie, 138
Down-Home Tuna Casserole, 111
Easy Stroganoff, 133
Family Night Noodle Bake, 116
Farm-Fresh Spinach Quiche, 144
Grandma's Stuffed Cabbage, 142
Grandma's Yankee Fried
    Chicken, 132
Layered Cabbage Rolls, 151
Mary's Noodle Bake, 113
Meatloaf, 139
Mom's Lazy Lasagna, 141
Mom's Spaghetti Sauce, 135
Old-Fashioned Meatballs, 134
Old-Fashioned Pork Chop
    Bake, 114
One-Pot Supper, 128
Pepper Steak, 145
Pork & Sauerkraut Supper, 130
Quick Chili Mac, 152
Reuben Casserole, 117
Scalloped Tomato Casserole, 122
Shepherd's Pie, 103
Shrimp with Garlic, 104
Sloppy Joes, 129
Smothered Steak, 131
Sour Cream Enchiladas, 112
Southwestern Chicken, 121
Spaghetti Pie, 110
Steak & Potatoes, 107
Stuffed Peppers, 148
Swiss Steak, 149
Turkey Casserole, 120

Salads

Banana Salad, 85
Caesar Salad, 98
Carrot & Raisin Salad, 81
Cherry Tomato Salad, 80
Chicken Salad, 99
Cookie Salad, 93
Cranberry Salad, 90
Family Reunion Fruit Salad, 100
Fruit Trifle Salad, 82
German Potato Salad, 157
Homemade Blue Cheese
    Dressing, 80
Marinated Vegetables, 96
Mom's Potato Salad, 88
Orange-Cranberry Salad, 92
Overnight Salad, 97
Red Potato Salad, 89
Ribbon Salad, 95
Shimmering Three-Berry
    Salad, 94
Sugar Snap Pea & Bean
    Salad, 91
Summertime Salad, 100
Summertime Spaghetti Salad, 79
Sunflower Salad, 84
Susie Salad, 86
Twelve-Layer Salad, 87
Vegetable Pasta Salad, 83
Vermicelli Salad, 81

Sides

Apple Valley Squash Casserole, 123
Birch Bayh Green Beans, 176
Brown Sugar Beans, 173
Butternut Squash, 178
Company Potatoes, 166
Copper Pennies, 172

Index

Corn & Tomatoes, 183
Cowboy Beans, 158
Creamy Broccoli Stuffing, 162
Escalloped Corn, 171
Family-Style Baked Beans, 155
Fruited Yams, 167
Garlic Smashed Potatoes, 179
Glorified Rice, 182
Grandma Leland's Red
   Cabbage, 174
Ham & Cauliflower Au Gratin, 156
Luke's Favorite Potatoes, 161
Macaroni Corn Casserole, 165
Marinated Vegetables, 177
Old-Fashioned Macaroni &
   Cheese, 159
Onion & Cheese Casserole, 108
Overnight Potato Casserole, 168
Red Beans & Rice Casserole, 105
Ruth's Rice Casserole, 119
Scalloped Potatoes, 163
Special Supper Stuffing, 164
Sweet Potato Casserole, 160
Vegetable Herb Trio, 170
Whipped Sweet Potatoes, 184
Zesty Broccoli, 180

Soups

Aunt Sandy's Special Chowder, 75
Barley Vegetable Soup, 60
Broccoli Cheddar Soup, 54
Broccoli Cheese Noodle Soup, 61
Camp Stew, 73
Cheesy Potato Soup, 64
Chicken Mulligan, 62
Corn & Sausage Chowder, 76
Country Chicken Stew, 53
Farmstead Split Pea Soup, 55
Fireside Chili, 70
Grandma's Chili, 56
Hearty Minestrone, 71
Homestyle Broccoli Soup, 69
Mama's Vegetable Beef Soup, 72
Minnesota Wild Rice Soup, 74
Norwegian Soup Au Gratin, 57
Old-Fashioned Beef Stew, 63
Onion Soup, 59
Senate Bean Soup, 67
Slow-Cooker Chicken Stew, 66
Tomato Bisque, 58
Traditional Wedding Soup, 68
Turkey-Vegetable Chowder, 65

Since 1992, we've been publishing country cookbooks for every kitchen and for every meal of the day! Each has hundreds of budget-friendly recipes, using ingredients you already have on hand. Their lay-flat binding makes them easy to use and each is filled with hand-drawn artwork and plenty of personality.

Send us your favorite recipe!

and the memory that makes it special for you!* If we select your recipe for a brand-new **Gooseberry Patch** cookbook, your name will appear right along with it...and you'll receive a FREE copy of the book.

Share your recipe on our website at www.gooseberrypatch.com

Or mail to:

Gooseberry Patch • Attn: Cookbook Dept.
PO Box 812 • Columbus, OH 43216-0812

* Don't forget to include your name, address, phone number and email address so we'll know how to reach you for your FREE book!

Find Gooseberry Patch wherever you are!

www.gooseberrypatch.com

Call us toll-free at 1•800•854•6673

U.S. to Canadian recipe equivalents

Volume Measurements

1/4 teaspoon	1 mL
1/2 teaspoon	2 mL
1 teaspoon	5 mL
1 tablespoon = 3 teaspoons	15 mL
2 tablespoons = 1 fluid ounce	30 mL
1/4 cup	60 mL
1/3 cup	75 mL
1/2 cup = 4 fluid ounces	125 mL
1 cup = 8 fluid ounces	250 mL
2 cups = 1 pint =16 fluid ounces	500 mL
4 cups = 1 quart	1 L

Weights

1 ounce	30 g
4 ounces	120 g
8 ounces	225 g
16 ounces = 1 pound	450 g

Oven Temperatures

300° F	150° C
325° F	160° C
350° F	180° C
375° F	190° C
400° F	200° C
450° F	230° C

Baking Pan Sizes

Square

8x8x2 inches	2 L = 20x20x5 cm
9x9x2 inches	2.5 L = 23x23x5 cm

Rectangular

13x9x2 inches	3.5 L = 33x23x5 cm

Loaf

9x5x3 inches	2 L = 23x13x7 cm

Round

8x1-1/2 inches	1.2 L = 20x4 cm
9x1-1/2 inches	1.5 L = 23x4 cm